**THE NEXT FRONTIER IN FERMENTING
AND HOME BREWING IS VINEGAR:
THE ESSENTIAL INGREDIENT FOR
ENHANCING YOUR HOME COOKING.**

Just about everyone has at least one bottle of vinegar in the pantry, but not many realize how much better the homemade kind tastes—the flavor is incomparable. And it's simple to make: all you need is a bottle of your favorite alcoholic beverage, a starter (or vinegar mother), and a few weeks of hands-off time.

Vinegar Revival shows you how to use homemade or store-bought vinegar to great effect with more than fifty recipes for drinks and cocktails (Strawberry Rhubarb Shrub, Switchel, Mint Vinegar Julep), pickles (Cured Grapes, Pickled Whole Garlic), sauces and vinaigrettes (Roasted Hot Sauce, Miso-Ginger Vinaigrette), mains and sides (Saucy Piquant Pork Chops, Roasted Red Cabbage), and dessert (Vinegar Pie, Balsamic Ice Cream). Whether you want to experiment with home brewing or just add some zing to your meals, this cookbook demystifies the process of making and tasting vinegar.

VINEGAR
REVIVAL

VINEGAR REVIVAL

ARTISANAL RECIPES FOR BRIGHTENING DISHES AND DRINKS WITH HOMEMADE VINEGARS

HARRY ROSENBLUM

PHOTOGRAPHS BY ED ANDERSON

CLARKSON POTTER/PUBLISHERS
New York

Library of Congress Cataloging-in-Publication Data

Names: Rosenblum, Harry, author.
Title: Vinegar revival : recipes for brightening dishes and drinks with
homemade vinegars / Harry Rosenblum ; photographs by Ed Anderson.
Description: First edition. | New York : Clarkson Potter/Publishers, 2017. |
Includes index.
Identifiers: LCCN 2016045694 | ISBN 9780451495037 (pbk.)
Subjects: LCSH: Cooking (Vinegar) | Vinegar. | LCGFT: Cookbooks.
Classification: LCC TX819.V5 R67 2017 | DDC 641.6/2—dc23
LC record available at https://lccn.loc.gov/2016045694

ISBN 978-0-451-49503-7

Ebook ISBN 978-0-451-49504-4

Printed in China

Interior and cover design by Marysarah Quinn
Interior and cover photographs by Ed Anderson

10 9 8 7 6 5 4 3 2 1

FIRST EDITION

TO MY MOTHER,
MARYLYN ROSENBLUM,
WHO WOULD HAVE BEEN
TERRIBLY PROUD

CONTENTS

||||||||||||||||||||||||||||||||

UNDERSTANDING
VINEGAR

Vinegar might be the most common ingredient in our pantries, but many of us don't know how to make use of this incredible acidic liquid. Sure, we mix it into salad dressings, and many folks have replaced their cleaning supplies with the distilled white stuff, but failing that, it hasn't yet found a place in our everyday cooking. Until now. When you have access to really good vinegar, you unlock flavor possibilities for cocktails, dinners, and even desserts. But you may not find great quality vinegars in your regular grocery store. For decades, bottled industrial acids have duped us into thinking we're buying malt or red wine vinegar. The liquid is brown or red, but it tastes nothing like beer or wine.

To have good-quality vinegar on hand, you just might have to make it yourself. But good news: it takes only three ingredients (including air), no special tools, and a little hands-off time. Use the best ingredients you can find—a locally made craft beer, in-season fruits and vegetables, wine that you would serve at the table—and you'll end up with a product so good you'll want to sip it straight. It's much easier to brew than beer or kombucha, and has many more uses. In the process, you'll save money, recycle potential waste, and completely change your cooking. Pour off a little from your master batch and give it to friends. You'll impress the hell out of them.

This book will walk you through the entire process of making vinegar, from start to sour finish. You'll learn all about the vinegar mother (page 12), what kinds of vinegars are easiest to make at home (page 27), and which ones you should just buy (page 30). You will also find fifty fantastic ways to make and enjoy vinegar, whether you're working with homemade or store-bought. Some of these are obvious uses (pickles, page 64) and others are more un-expected (Mint Vinegar Julep, page 60, or Vinegar Pie, page 137). Many of the recipes call for specific types of vinegar; however, you should feel free to experiment and explore. If a recipe specifies apple cider vinegar and all you have is red wine vinegar, give it a shot—by no means are these recipes com-pletely prescriptive. Play around with whatever you have on hand.

MY ACID TRIP

I first caught the fermentation bug in the mid-1990s while a student at Hampshire College in Amherst, Massachusetts. Since beer was illegal for me to buy, but the ingredients to make it weren't, I learned to brew my own. When I moved to Brooklyn after college, I set out to continue my fermenta-tion experiments. There was a problem though: New York City had no easily accessible home-brew stores, and I couldn't get packages delivered to my apartment. Once I realized that packets of dry yeast would fit through the mail slot, I ordered dry wine and champagne yeast and began fermenting cider I'd pick up at the Union Square Greenmarket.

Then in 2005, while preparing to bottle a five-gallon batch of cider, I discovered homemade vinegar. When I was almost finished bottling, I real-ized I hadn't saved enough empty bottles for the whole five gallons. I did, however, have a gallon jug, and I remembered that a bottle of organic white wine vinegar in my pantry had grown this odd-looking round raft at the top of the liquid—a vinegar "mother." I'd read a little about how vinegar was made, and so I filled the jug with the rest of the cider, plopped in the mother from the donor jar, and left the open jug in a corner of my dark boiler room for a few months. When I remembered to check on it, I found that the cider had turned to vinegar—and it was delicious. In fact, it tasted better than the cider I had started with.

Motivated to try my hand at making other vinegars, I begged my friends at the Brooklyn Brewery for five gallons of just-finished beer to make my own malt vinegar. Real vinegar made from good beer was a revelation. Unlike most of the commercial malt varieties, which are made from malted barley or corn and get their color from caramel, my malt vinegar was complex, earthy, toasty, malty and tangy. It mimicked the flavors of the original brew—and was a perfect accompaniment for everything from seltzer to fries. I've been experimenting making other vinegars ever since (spruce, fruit, wine, foraged berries, melon, and more), and now more than ten years and dozens of vinegars later, I still get a thrill from a finished batch. You start with something so seemingly normal and, through what feels like culinary alchemy, it turns into a delicious and satisfying ingredient.

THE SOUR PROCESS

Vinegar is the next naturally occurring step in the fermentation process after you make beverages like beer and wine. When the alcohol in these delicious drinks comes into contact with a microorganism called acetobacter and there's oxygen present, the bacteria consume the ethanol and produce acetic acid, which is the sour component in vinegar. It may sound complicated, but it's a very easy process. Even better, acetobacters are found just about anywhere in the environment. They collect and prosper in places where ethanol naturally occurs, such as when wild yeasts colonize the nectar in flowers or the skins of rotting fruits and begin fermenting the sugars into alcohol.

Though the word *vinegar* derives from the French for "sour wine," vinegar can be made from much more than wine. Fruit Vinegar (page 33) uses a traditional method that's especially popular in warm climates, and it's a great way to turn your scraps into something sublime. Alongside the classic wine vinegars, you'll find unusual ones made from sorghum, persimmon, tomato, maple syrup, ramps, grapefruit, or honey. If people can eat it or drink it and it has sugar, then it can be made into vinegar. The key ingredient you need to make great vinegar is a sugary or alcoholic base. But remember that acetobacters need more than just the ethanol to make the conversion of alcohol into acetic acid; other minerals and nutrients are required. The carbohydrates, sugars, tannins, and nutrients in wine and beer help the bacteria thrive. Darker beers, red wines, meads, and ciders, which have more nutrients and tannins, tend to make better vinegars more easily and stand up to the variances present in home fermentation. More subtle white wine and sake usually work well, too, but they may require some tweaking and experimentation to get your fermentations exactly right.

THE MOTHER

Just as our mothers are often the most important people in our lives, the same can be said for vinegar making. What we call the *vinegar mother* is a collection of slimy cellulose that forms at the intersection of the base liquid and the air. It's a by-product of the bacteria converting the alcohol into acetic acid—and a good thing! Think of it as a visual cue that the conversion of the main ingredient into "live" vinegar is actually happening. In most cases, your homemade vinegar will develop a sizable mother, which only increases as you start making larger batches. A five-gallon batch will often yield two-plus pounds of mother.

Keep your mother healthy; you don't want her to drown. She should float on top and be uniform thickness and rubbery to the touch. Over time she may have babies that grow on top as she starts to sink. When that happens, you'll want to pull out any mother that sinks and either start a new batch of vinegar or give a piece of it to your friends as a starter.

Mother will continue to grow on healthy vinegar; if you leave a jar long enough, the vinegar will evaporate leaving a jar full of mother and her babies—and they'll just keep growing. So it's important to pour off and bottle your vinegar for use once it's completely acidified.

TASTING VINEGAR

Whether you're sampling your own homemade vinegar or are in the market for a quality bottle, you'll want to know what to look for when taste testing. (Wine vinegars can cost $40 a liter or more at the store; for the price of one decent bottle of wine you can make more than a liter of top-notch vinegar for under $15.) Quality vinegar should taste bright, with the acid clear on your tongue and in the back of your throat, especially with stronger vinegars. Because acid can burn you, don't take a shot of vinegar without first tasting a small sip to see how it feels. The smell and flavor should be reminiscent of the vinegar's base—sherry vinegar should taste like sherry, red wine vinegar like red wine, et cetera. Try a blind tasting of a base product and then its vinegar counterpart. See if you can pair them up. If it's good quality, it should be an easy match.

Much like drinking a fine wine or craft beer, focus on being open to the act of tasting, allowing your brain to work on what your nose and tongue are taking in from the vinegar. Take a tiny sip, and let it sit on the front of your tongue while you breathe in to aerate it. This will give you the full flavor and acid of the vinegar. As it settles on your tongue, notice the flavors; a good vinegar will taste lively and more flavorful than just a strong hit of acid. Let your mind consider what you'd use it on, or if this one is right for the dish you're working on tonight.

If you're tasting a whole range of vinegars to compare and discuss, take a sugar cube, dip it in the vinegar, and suck the vinegar from the cube. I find that this helps you identify the flavor of the base, because your tongue isn't bombarded by the acid in the presence of sugar. If you're into scientific recording and note taking, keep a small book and write down notes on your own vinegars as well as others that you taste.

DISTILLED WHITE VINEGAR

If what you're after is just a clear acid for pickling or cleaning, then buying cheap store-bought distilled white vinegar is for you. Manufactured in giant acetators, distilled to clear purity, and then watered down, this industrial acid is edible and food safe. (Acetators are large pieces of equipment that control the temperature and oxygen levels while mixing the vinegar to convert it from alcohol into vinegar as fast as possible; the vinegar is then distilled to remove any impurities and watered down to a standard 5 percent acidity.) Whereas the acidity and pH (power of hydrogen) of homemade vinegar may vary from one batch to the next (more on this on page 150), store-bought distilled vinegar is the same every time, so you can be sure your pickles are safely canned.

Here are some ideas for using up that gallon:

1 Pickle something (see page 64).

2 Impress your kids with a volcano: Place a jar on the ground outside and add a ¼ cup of baking soda in the jar. Add 10 drops of red food coloring. Pour in 1 cup of vinegar and watch the lava erupt!

3 Wash your fruit with a 1:1 vinegar-to-water solution to make it last longer and remove wax and other residue.

4 Use the same mix to clean your floor, sink, and tub.

5 A 50:50 vinegar-to-water solution or full-strength vinegar will keep ants away; simply spray it where you see them.

6 Neutralize pet odors and accidents by spraying the area with a 50:50 vinegar-to-water solution after drying or soaking up as much as possible.

7 Bring a spray bottle of vinegar to the beach in case of jellyfish stings and to relieve minor sunburn.

COOK BRIGHTER AND BETTER

Even though we consume some form of vinegar every day (in the condiments, dressings, and pickles we eat), vinegar by itself is still an underappreciated ingredient that can transform your cooking and your eating. In many cases, the punch of the acid plays off the richness of the dish, adding a level of complexity and lightness to heavy foods such as organ meats and thick sauces. It can also serve as a clean note that finishes braised greens or pushes almost any soup (like My Onion Soup on page 114) from mediocre to delicious. As an experiment, sprinkle vinegar on dishes you normally wouldn't. Not in a we-just-won-the-World-Series-champagne kind of way, but deliberately enough to taste it with the food. Try your scrambled eggs with a little vinegar. Taste your cooked rice plain, and then put some vinegar on it. Take a bite of your sautéed kale, then finish it with some vinegar. You'll notice such a difference in the dish that I wouldn't be surprised if you started enjoying it on everything.

NONREACTIVE COOKWARE

Cast iron, wood, steel, and aluminum can react with the acid in vinegar and leech off flavors into your food, which is why many of the recipes in this book call for using nonreactive cookware or bowls. Feel free to use enameled, stainless steel, ceramic, or glass, depending on the recipe and your preference. It is worth noting that, historically, people cooked with vinegar in cast iron all the time because it was their only option, so if your cast-iron skillet or Dutch oven is well seasoned, go ahead and use it, just make sure to remove the food to a platter or bowl when it's done cooking to minimize any reaction.

DRINK IN THE RAW

The vinegar you make at home is a living liquid. The bacteria producing the acetic acid are constantly eating, living, and reproducing. If you're looking for the most probiotic of vinegars to consume for health, then you have to make your own, as it will have lots of trace minerals, enzymes, and other compounds that won't be present in large-scale commercially produced vinegar, especially distilled. Making your own is the only true way to ensure that what you're consuming is, in fact, alive.

While there are many natural vinegars on the market that are unpasteurized, this does not mean that acetobacters are living in the bottle. At some point, the living bacteria count in the bottle will fall as they die off from lack of oxygen. While vinegar never really goes bad (it's its own preservative), you will still see "best by" or "use by" dates on commercially produced bottles. Keep in mind that the closer you are to that date, the longer the vinegar has been in the bottle and therefore has less living bacteria. The taste will change over time as well, and you may want to explore aging batches of your own vinegar to taste the changes.

Researchers believe that the amino acids present in live vinegar are related to its medicinal qualities. These amino acids help reduce lactic-acid buildup in the blood, which has been correlated to fatigue, irritability, stiffness, and soreness. "Old-timers" in many cultures take a daily tonic of vinegar, often sweetened with honey, maple syrup, or another traditional sugar, to help stay healthy. Vinegar helps keep hypertension in check and regulates blood sugar and body pH. Though it's not a quick fix or cure-all, I try to drink an ounce of live vinegar every morning in a glass of seltzer. I find it refreshing and delicious.

Vinegar can be used on the skin to regulate the acidity and clean away dead cells as well as keep away bacteria, fungus, and microbes. Washing your face and hair in a solution of ½ cup of vinegar diluted in 4 cups of water will help clear makeup, hair-care products, and other residue and limit dandruff and peeling skin. Vinegar can also be used to treat acne and acts as a natural astringent to balance oily or dry skin.

There's science to suggest that the bacterial makeup of our own bodies relates to our levels of happiness and stress, which can contribute to preventing (or causing) cancer. While you may not be able to pinpoint any direct effects of consuming raw vinegar on a daily basis, I can tell you that consuming something you've made yourself will contribute to your sense of accomplishment, happiness, and self-sufficiency.

BEFORE YOU START

Vinegar is simple to make at home, and the final result will be unlike anything you can buy. While the process is easy to master, with these tools and troubleshooting tips, your first batch will be successful.

TOOLS TO HAVE ON HAND

You probably already have the basic supplies for making vinegar in your kitchen. The more you get into vinegar making, the more you might want to invest in a better vessel (see Resources, page 153) or pH testing supplies (see Resources, page 153). But for now you'll just need these:

- **A vessel** to hold liquid during fermentation: glass, wood, stoneware, even food-safe plastic. Those glass lemonade dispensers with a spigot near the bottom are perfect for drawing off finished vinegar.
- **Cheesecloth** or a cotton tea towel to cover the opening of the vessel.

THE WINE THIEF

I love using a wine thief for sampling vinegar. This optional, handy tool allows you to pull out a little vinegar without disturbing the mother.

BARREL CARE

Stemming from the wine-making tradition, oak barrels were the obvious vessel of choice for aging and making vinegar in Europe (see Orléans Method, page 30); after aging a wine, the barrels are often discarded. So what better way to reuse them than to make vinegar? Now you'll find smaller oak barrels sold especially for vinegar brewing—some of them sit on their side and some are upright, but each has a spigot at the bottom for drawing off your finished product.

When you get your oak barrel you'll need to prep it before starting your vinegar. Simply fill the barrel with water and let the wood soak and swell. The swelling should seal any leaks in about twenty-four hours. Remove the water and begin the process for making the Small Batch Vinegar (page 25) or Never-Ending Vinegar (page 29).

If you're brewing a single batch of vinegar, once you've bottled the vinegar, you can rinse the barrel out to remove any extra sediment and start your next batch of vinegar. There's no need to add any additional mother, as the acetobacters are now living in the wood of the barrel. Don't use a vinegar barrel to age wine, spirits, or beer—once you put the bacteria in there you can't really get them out.

To store your barrel for a prolonged period of time, fill it completely with water mixed with 1 teaspoon of citric acid and 1½ teaspoons of potassium metabisulfite (you can find both at home-brewing stores) for every gallon of barrel volume. Stored this way, the barrel should keep indefinitely. When you're ready to use the barrel again, rinse it well and add additional mother to the recipe.

TROUBLESHOOTING

Washing and drying is usually all you need to do for tools and vessels made of hard materials like metal and glass, whereas permeable things like wood barrels need to be treated a little differently (see page 21). While you don't need to use sanitizer like you do with beer brewing, working in a clean environment will help you succeed every time you make vinegar and prevent batches from spoiling.

When you have a batch that goes bad, try to figure out where you went wrong.

• Was the fermentation vessel not cleaned properly?
Residue left over from something that was previously in the vessel can infect your vinegar batch with off flavors or even mold. Never use a barrel or bucket that has been used to hold nonfood items.

• Was the vinegar stored in too warm a space? Or too cold?
Heat over 100°F or below 60°F will cause the acetobacters to go dormant. Try to store your brewing vinegar in a dark place that's around 70–95°F.

• Do you notice too many fruit flies?
A few fruit flies is to be expected, but sometimes they'll breed like crazy and you'll have a barrel full of them. While not harmful it is off-putting. You can strain the vinegar through a sieve or cheesecloth, clean the vessel, and keep it going, or you can throw it out and start over.

• Are there vinegar eels?
Vinegar eels, called *Turbatrix aceti*, are tiny nematode worms about 1/16 of an inch long that live and feed on the vinegar mother. You will sometimes find them in raw vinegar. They are harmless and can be strained out with a sieve or cheesecloth; you can also pasteurize your finished vinegar (see page 149) to kill them.

• Was the original wine corked?
Corked wine is wine that has gone bad in the bottle. It will smell like wet cardboard and taste thin. While people often confuse this with a wine "going to vinegar" given the lack of oxygen and the alcohol content of

the wine, the chances of wine spontaneously turning to vinegar in the bottle is very unlikely. Make sure you taste the wine before beginning your vinegar process.

• Is your wood barrel giving the vinegar an off-flavor?

The wood in your brand-new oak barrel will leech a little into your vinegar. While it's possible for your vinegar to become "over oaked," with time and extended use the wood flavors of a barrel will mellow. If you're not happy with the finished vinegar, you may want to start over with a new batch until your barrel becomes seasoned.

• Did the vinegar develop a yeast infection?

Yeasts are in the air and if one takes hold of your vinegar it can grow on top of the liquid and have a bread-like smell. I've had a few cases of a yeast called *kahm* growing in my vinegar, which looks like a white veil that turns into a thick wrinkled mass with a waxy texture. Skim off any visible yeast, so that your acetobacters can take over. You can add some finished vinegar to lower the pH of your batch and make the environment inhospitable to the yeast.

• Is there mold?

If you see green, black, or white hairy mold on your vinegar or mother skim it off. If it comes back then you should throw out the batch and start over. Because it needs oxygen to thrive, it will grow only on the surface and can't grow in liquid.

• Is there too much or too little alcohol?

If you use any base with an alcohol content above 9 percent it will be difficult for the acetobacters to thrive and prosper. Use anything below 3 percent and they won't have enough food to survive. Choose a base with an ABV (alcohol by volume) between 4 percent and 7 percent and they'll be just right.

Every batch of homemade vinegar can turn out differently, which is what makes home brewing so interesting. As a home fermenter, I don't care about making the same batch every time, but if you're so inclined, keep a notebook to track your vinegar experiments. You may even want to save a small bottle from each batch, so you can have vertical tastings of your own vintages.

MASTER
VINEGARS,
INFUSIONS,
AND SHRUBS

This chapter outlines the basics of vinegar making and is a great place to start if you're interested in creating your own. Any of the infusions and the shrubs (fruit- and vinegar-based sugar syrups also known as drinking vinegars) included are delicious in cocktails as well as in food and shouldn't be limited to one use or the other. If you've got a hankering for making vinegar out of unusual ingredients (cider with port, pear juice with bourbon), then by all means give it a shot. At worst you'll watch a ferment fail before you throw out about a liter of liquid and move on to the next one. At best you'll make a sublime vinegar to share with your friends and enjoy on your food. If you don't have the time or patience to make your own, any of the recipes on pages 31–144 can always be made with store-bought vinegar (buy the best that you can find).

SMALL BATCH VINEGAR

MAKES ABOUT 1½ QUARTS

There are two ways to make vinegar; both are delicious but involve slightly different timelines. If you want to brew and bottle a single batch from your favorite wine, beer, cider, or sake so that the vinegar will have the characteristics of that single base, then follow this recipe. If what you're after is something more flexible that you can continue to add to and have available for use at any time—and you don't care about it having a specific flavor profile—then start your vinegar in a vessel with a spigot and refer to the Never-Ending Vinegar method on page 29.

1 (750ml) bottle of good wine (red, white, or rosé), or an equivalent amount of beer, hard cider, or sake (see Variations on page 27)

½ cup vinegar mother or live raw vinegar

TIP: WHEN TO ADD WATER

If your starting fermented product has an ABV of 8 percent or lower (like hard cider or beer), you will not need to add water to it. Just throw it and the mother into the jar and begin. For a higher-alcohol wine or sake, you can add a 1:1 ratio of water to wine—just make sure you choose the right-sized vessel for fermentation to allow for the extra water.

1. Open the wine and taste it to make sure the bottle is good and not corked (corked wine smells like wet cardboard and tastes thin). Pour the bottle into a half-gallon jar with a wide mouth, seal the jar, and shake well to aerate the wine and get the wine ready for acetic fermentation.

2. Add water until the jar is three-fourths full (any drinking water is fine; see Tip). Add the mother, cover the mouth of the jar with cheesecloth or fabric, and seal it with a rubber band to keep out pests. Leave the jar in a dark corner at room temperature for 3 to 4 weeks, checking regularly to see that a mother is growing on the surface and things look mold-free. There is no need to ever shake or stir the mixture after step 1; you don't want to disturb the mother or she'll sink. Give it a sniff; you should start to smell vinegar!

3. After 2 months, taste the vinegar for acidity and bask in the delicious work the millions of bacteria have done for you. Strain out the mother and bottle the vinegar, reserving the mother for another

RECIPE CONTINUES

use. Start using the vinegar immediately, or age the vinegar for a year or more to mellow the flavors (see page 151).

4. Begin a new batch with your mother, or give some of it away as a starter.

NOTE: It may take more or less time for your vinegar to completely convert from alcohol. Differences in local humidity and temperature, as well as the exact nutrients in the wine you choose to start with, will all affect your timeline. Taste the vinegar every week or so to better understand the progress.

MAKE VINEGAR FASTER

If you're too impatient to wait for your finished vinegar, you can speed up the process by aerating, or adding air to your vinegar. By providing more surface area and frequent contact between the liquid and the air, you actively feed the mother or acetobacter, allowing the acetic acid conversion to happen more quickly. I've come across people experimenting with all kinds of methods—from using fish tank air pumps, to oxygen bottles, to slow moving agitators that can cut down the timeline to 10 or so days.

RED WINE VINEGAR

This is the staple in any vinegar lover's arsenal. There are lots of industrially produced red wine vinegars that taste acidic and look like they used to be red wine, but they pale in comparison to what you can make at home. This is why red wine vinegar is a great place to start your home fermentations, as your homemade stuff will blow away almost anything you can buy.

WHITE WINE VINEGAR

A great go-to for herb infusions, this variety is often harder to turn into vinegar at home than red. The lack of tannins seems to affect the bacteria's ability to convert the alcohol and thrive. I've had about a 50 percent success rate with making white wine vinegar at home. The flavor of the finished product will be subtler than red, and its clean brightness is welcome in everything from cocktails to soup.

ROSÉ VINEGAR

Rosé wine yields very light pink vinegar that looks beautiful in the bottle. With more tannins than white wine (from skin contact during fermentation), it should present few problems in converting to acid.

APPLE CIDER VINEGAR

When you set out to make cider vinegar, you need to decide whether you want to make it from fresh juice or already fermented hard cider. If you live in an area known for its apples and have access to good-quality fresh pressed apple cider, or can get good apples to press yourself and you're into home brewing, then I highly recommend researching and fermenting your own hard cider first and then converting it to vinegar, or going for a simultaneous fermentation (see page 151). Otherwise buy the best hard cider you can and proceed; however, note that the lower alcohol in hard cider eliminates the need to water it down, so add your mother and hard cider, skip the water, and vinegar is in your future.

MALT (BEER) VINEGAR

Here's vinegar that will really up your game, and it's quite possibly the easiest to make. Sometimes called *alegar* (ale vinegar), malt vinegar is most often associated with the British Isles as the chief dressing for fish-and-chips (see Fish and Latkes, page 117). Commercially, malt vinegar is most often made from things that aren't really beer (usually no hops and not really brewed), and once you make your own, you'll be floored by the delicious results. The best malt vinegar begins with a medium to dark beer that you like; light pilsners and lagers are somewhat bland to drink and will yield blander vinegar. I like a brown ale, porter, or anything that's not super hoppy. Since most beers are under 9 percent alcohol by volume (ABV) and full of nutrients and tannins, they're perfect for making vinegar without needing dilution.

RICE (SAKE) VINEGAR

There are many rice "wines" in the marketplace (though sake is really a brewed product more akin to beer than wine, we call it wine in the United States because its ABV tends to be more like wine or even higher—in the 16 to 17 percent range). As with everything else, start with a sake you like to drink. This will likely be the lightest vinegar you can make, both in color and flavor, as most rice wines tend to have a very light and subtle flavor.

NEVER-ENDING VINEGAR

This method benefits from an oak vinegar barrel or ceramic jug with a spigot (see page 19 or 20). This is the type of home production you might encounter in a kitchen in the South of France or at an Italian *nonna*'s house. In this version you add the last few ounces of wine from the previous evening's bottle directly to the cask with a little water, skim off the mother once in a while so the spigot doesn't get clogged, and decant the vinegar every month or so into a bottle for use. This is a grand mixture of all the wines you drink—white, red, and rosé included—and you also can add beer, sherry, port, hard cider, or any alcoholic beverage. The result is more of a farmhouse mixture and an economical way to turn those last drops of anything into something amazing. One benefit here is that the bacteria should be very healthy and convert the alcohol rather quickly since you keep feeding them similar to a sourdough starter. Note that every time you draw off some vinegar, it will be different from the previous time. So if you're a stickler for the consistency of taste, follow the Small Batch Vinegar recipe (page 25).

---

1 quart of Small Batch Vinegar (page 25) or store-bought raw vinegar

Leftover wine, beer, sherry, hard cider, or port

STORING VINEGAR AND THE MOTHER

As long as you keep your bottle of homemade vinegar well sealed, out of sunlight, and away from heat, it should last for months or even years. Discard it if you notice an off-flavor or bad smell when you open it. Store any leftover mother in a tightly closed jar or container in the fridge until you're ready to give it away or add it to your next batch.

1. Once your vinegar finishes brewing, add it to a 1 to 2-gallon barrel or crock with a spigot if you haven't already.

2. Draw off the finished vinegar as needed and start regularly feeding the bacteria in the vessel with fresh wine, beer, sake—whatever. Add water as needed (see Tip, page 25). Every few months, remove the mass of the mother that forms so it doesn't overwhelm the barrel. Save the mother for another batch, give some away, or just toss it out. You'll have plenty more in the near future.

3. Let your taste buds be your guide when you draw off vinegar for use. If it doesn't taste acidic enough, then pour the vinegar back in the barrel and taste it again in a week or two.

ORLÉANS METHOD

The Orléans method—named for the city in France where vinegar was first commercialized in the fourteenth century—is a traditional style of vinegar making using oak barrels turned on their sides. Holes are drilled into the barrels to promote airflow, and the barrels are filled halfway with diluted wine. Muslin covers the barrels to prevent pests, and the wine is left to ferment and mature until it reaches the proper acidity, anywhere from four to eighteen months. About three-fourths of the finished live vinegar is then drawn off, leaving the remainder in the barrel, which is refilled with more diluted wine. This process is essentially the same one we follow now in most home vinegar making; while you can choose to make vinegar in a crock, jar, jug, bottle, or barrel, the basic process is the same: we're taking wine or other alcohol and leaving it to turn into vinegar by exposure to air in a contained environment.

TWO VINEGARS TO BUY, NOT MAKE

SHERRY VINEGAR. Unless you live in Spain, have access to a *solera*, and have twelve years to wait, you'll ultimately be disappointed with what you make at home. The solera is a series of rows of barrels used in sherry making, where the wine (or vinegar) is moved from one row down to the next as it ferments and ages; by the time it reaches the end of the bottom row, it's sherry vinegar. The controls and the history of sherry and sherry vinegar make it one of the best and most reliable to buy, and the experts really do it right. You can add sherry to your Never-Ending Vinegar (page 29) for a great flavor variation, and buy some good sherry vinegar to keep in your pantry and get to the cooking part of this book.

BALSAMIC VINEGAR. Balsamic was really the first "gourmet" vinegar on the market when gourmet foods began to catch on in the 1970s in the United States. Putting balsamic vinegar and olive oil on the table became the benchmark of any dinner party host's worldliness. As such they were also soon overtaken by commodity imposters, and you can now find cheap so-called balsamic in the grocery store alongside cheap maybe-not-really-olive oil. Good-quality balsamic vinegar is nuanced, sweet, tangy, and viscous. Like sherry vinegar, unless you've got years, a large space, and deep pockets, making the real thing at home is not worth doing. Instead, support the great work of the fine folks in Reggio Emilia and Modena.

HONEY VINEGAR

MAKES ABOUT 2 QUARTS

Honey is one of the most natural sugars and has so many nuanced flavors. Converting that to an acidic ingredient works for various culinary applications—in vinaigrettes and as a general table condiment are my favorites, and I know this one will find its way into drinks and sweets as soon as you make it. The grapefruit called for here adds needed nutrients and counteracts the antimicrobial effects of the honey, allowing the yeast to ferment the sugars into alcohol.

2 pounds honey (see Tip)

½ grapefruit, flesh and skin cut into strips

¼ teaspoon (2.5g) champagne yeast (see Tip)

¼ cup homemade apple cider vinegar (see page 27), or store-bought

TIP

Champagne yeast comes in a 5-gram packet, which is enough to make 5 gallons of wine. You can find champagne yeast at any home brewing supply store or online.

1. Add the honey to a stockpot with ½ gallon of water. Bring to a simmer over medium heat, stirring until the honey dissolves.

2. Squeeze the juice from the grapefruit slices into the pot, then add the flesh and skin. Remove the pot from the heat.

3. Let the liquid cool to room temperature, then strain it into a gallon jug or jar. Add the champagne yeast and the vinegar. Cover the jar with cheesecloth and seal with a rubber band. Leave the jar in a dark corner for 3 to 4 weeks, checking regularly to see that a mother is growing on the surface and things look mold-free.

4. Check the vinegar after 4 weeks by tasting it for acidity (the mixture may take up to 3 months to fully convert to vinegar). Strain out the mother and bottle the vinegar, reserving the mother for another use. Start using the vinegar immediately, or age the vinegar for a year or more to mellow the flavors.

5. Begin a new batch with your mother, or give some of it away as a starter.

FRUIT VINEGAR

MAKES ABOUT 1 PINT

Many cultures have a long history of making fruit vinegars, including strawberry, blueberry, fig, persimmon, and pear. Pineapple is one of the most common vinegars in both Mexico and Central America, as well as in Southeast Asia. This recipe is easily scalable: just double or triple the ingredients. You can also make vinegar with just fruit scraps (peels and cores), but know that the flavor will be different if you're not using the flesh.

1 pound fresh fruit or fruit scraps (the peels, flesh, and/or cores), cut into small pieces

⅓ cup sugar

½ cup live unpasteurized vinegar, such as homemade red wine vinegar (page 27) or apple cider vinegar (page 27), or store-bought

TIP

You can make this recipe with many other flavoring agents as well; I've used both spruce tips and cantaloupe skins. Use the same proportions: ⅓ cup sugar to 4 cups of your product, and water to cover. If your fermentation doesn't start after 3 days, add champagne yeast (see page 31).

1. To a ½ gallon mason jar, add the fruit and sugar. Add water to cover the fruit and pour in the starter vinegar. Cover the mouth of the vessel with cheesecloth and secure with a rubber band.

2. Stir the mixture once a day for the first week, at which point the natural yeasts on the skins of the fruit will start to ferment the sugars into alcohol. Let the fruit ferment for another week, stirring occasionally. It should be bubbling lightly as the yeast ferments the sugars into ethanol and releases carbon dioxide.

3. Remove the cheesecloth, strain out and discard the solids, and add the liquid back to the jar to ferment into vinegar. Cover again with the cheesecloth.

4. Check the vinegar after 4 weeks (it may take up to 3 months to fully convert), taste the vinegar for acidity. Strain out the mother and bottle the vinegar, reserving the mother for another use. Start using the vinegar immediately, or age the vinegar for a year or more to mellow the flavors.

5. Begin a new batch with your mother, or give some of it away as a starter.

INFUSED VINEGARS

Adding flavorful ingredients to homemade or store-bought vinegars creates a simple infusion that punches up the flavor, and makes for more interesting salad dressings or mayonnaise. Infused vinegars also make great gifts. All of the following recipes assume 1 pint (2 cups) of vinegar for the infusion, but you can scale them as necessary for larger amounts. If you are making an infusion to give away, note that including a sprig of fresh herb in the bottle may look nice at first, but eventually the colors of the herb will fade and look rather wan, so if you're gifting any of these infusions, you're better off opting for an interesting bottle to give a visual boost instead of the sprig in the bottle. Infused vinegars will keep for months at room temperature. The flavors may fade over time, but they will never spoil.

SHISO VINEGAR
MAKES 1 PINT

1 pint homemade apple cider vinegar (page 27), or store-bought

¼ cup packed fresh green shiso leaves (about 20; see Tip), measured and cut into chiffonade

TIP

Green shiso, also called *perilla*, is an herb that is similar to basil. It can be found at most Asian grocery stores.

1. In a small nonreactive saucepan over medium heat, heat the vinegar to just below a simmer (about 160°F). Add the shiso to a clean pint-sized mason jar with a tight-fitting lid, and then pour in the warm vinegar. Screw on the lid and store at room temperature for up to a month.

2. When the flavor is to your liking, strain out and discard the solids and transfer the vinegar to a clean narrow-mouth glass bottle with a cork or lid for storage and use. The vinegar will keep tightly sealed at room temperature for up to 6 months.

TARRAGON AND BLACK PEPPER VINEGAR

MAKES 1 PINT

1 pint homemade white wine vinegar
(page 27), or store-bought

2 (8-inch) tarragon sprigs

12 whole black peppercorns

2 allspice berries

1. In a small nonreactive saucepan over medium heat, heat the vinegar to just below a simmer (about 160°F). Add the tarragon, peppercorns, and allspice to a clean pint-sized mason jar with a tight-fitting lid, then pour in the warm vinegar. Screw on the lid and store at room temperature for up to 1 month.

2. When the flavor is to your liking, strain out and discard the solids and transfer the vinegar to a clean narrow-mouth glass bottle with a cork or lid for storage and use. The vinegar will keep tightly sealed at room temperature for up to 6 months.

HOT PEPPER VINEGAR
MAKES 1 PINT

**1 pint homemade white wine vinegar
(page 27) or apple cider vinegar
(page 27), or store-bought**

**3 to 8 dried peppers of your choice
(I prefer Calabrian; see Tip)**

1. In a small nonreactive saucepan
over medium heat, heat the vinegar
to just below a simmer (about
160°F). Place the peppers in a clean
pint-sized mason jar with a tight-
fitting lid, then pour in the warm
vinegar (there's no need to shake
the mixture). Screw on the lid and
store at room temperature.

2. The flavor will develop over the
first few weeks. When the flavor is
to your liking, you can strain the
vinegar into a clean narrow-mouth
glass bottle with a cork or lid for
storage and use. The vinegar
will keep tightly sealed at room
temperature for up to 6 months.

TIP: The heat of this infusion really
depends on the peppers you're using. You
can always thin it out with more vinegar
if you find it too spicy. Use the pickled
peppers in soup or chili.

EARL GREY VINEGAR
MAKES 1 PINT

1 pint homemade red wine vinegar (page 27), or store-bought

2 Earl Grey tea bags or 2 teaspoons loose Earl Grey tea leaves

1. In a small nonreactive saucepan over medium heat, heat the vinegar just below boiling (about 200°F). Place the tea in a medium nonreactive bowl and pour the warm vinegar over it.

2. Infuse for 5 minutes and strain out the solids, discard, and pour the vinegar into a clean narrow-mouth glass bottle with a cork or lid for storage and use. The vinegar will keep tightly sealed at room temperature for up to 6 months.

GETTING HIGH ON ACID

So far, I haven't found a way to infuse cannabis directly into vinegar. If all you're after is just the flavor, and not the other benefits of the cannabis, you can substitute raw cannabis for shiso in the recipe on page 34. Cannabinoids are fat or alcohol soluble, not acid soluble, and you have to heat the cannabis first (240°F for 15 minutes should do the trick) to activate. For an easy edible, you can make cannabis-infused olive oil and then use it in a vinaigrette (page 86), or you could make a tincture with high-proof alcohol and add that to your vinegars.

GREEN TEA VINEGAR
MAKES 1 PINT

1 pint homemade white wine vinegar (page 27), or store-bought

2 tablespoons high-quality sencha green tea leaves

1. In a small nonreactive saucepan over medium heat, heat the vinegar to just below boiling (about 200°F). Place the tea in a medium nonreactive bowl and pour the warm vinegar over it. Let the vinegar infuse for 5 minutes.

2. Strain out the tea leaves, which are now pickled, and save them for adding to a rice or grain bowl (see Tip). Pour the vinegar into a clean narrow-mouth glass bottle with a cork or lid for storage and use. The vinegar will keep tightly sealed at room temperature for up to 6 months.

TIP: Use this infusion in place of the dashi vinegar in the Sumeshi (Sushi Rice) Bowl (page 133) or the Seaweed Salad (page 107) for a vegan option.

DASHI VINEGAR

MAKES 1 PINT

2 cups store-bought distilled white vinegar or homemade rice (sake) vinegar (page 27), or store-bought

1 ounce shredded kombu

½ cup packed bonito flakes

1. In a small nonreactive saucepan, combine the vinegar and kombu and bring to a simmer over medium heat. Simmer the kombu for 3 minutes, then strain it out. For the best flavor, do not boil the kombu.

2. Remove the saucepan from the heat and stir in the bonito flakes. Let stand for 2 minutes and strain the vinegar into a clean narrow-mouth glass bottle with a cork or lid for storage and use; discard the bonito flakes. The vinegar will keep tightly sealed at room temperature for up to 6 months.

LEMON ZEST AND BASIL VINEGAR

MAKES 1 PINT

1 pint homemade white wine vinegar (page 27), or store-bought

Zest of 1 lemon, cut in ¼- to ½-inch-wide strips (see Tips)

6 basil leaves

1. In a small nonreactive saucepan over medium heat, heat the vinegar to just below boiling (about 200°F). Place the lemon zest and basil in a pint-sized mason jar and pour in the hot vinegar. Let cool; cover and infuse overnight at room temperature.

2. Strain out and discard the solids and pour the vinegar into a clean narrow-mouth glass bottle with a cork or lid for storage and use. The vinegar will keep tightly sealed at room temperature for up to 6 months.

TIPS: Try to avoid using the bitter white pith of the lemon peel.

You can also make a shrub or drinking vinegar out of this infusion—a splash of shrub is much more refreshing in water than just a squeeze of lemon. Just add 1 cup of sugar to the vinegar and simmer to dissolve the sugar.

CHIVE BLOSSOM VINEGAR
MAKES 1 PINT

12 chive blossoms, or more as desired

1 pint store-bought distilled white vinegar or homemade white wine vinegar (page 27), or store-bought

1. Place the chive blossoms in a clean pint-sized mason jar with a tight-fitting lid and pour the vinegar over them. Cover and let the jar stand at room temperature for 5 days.

2. Strain out the blossoms, which are now pickled, and save them for tossing in salads or sautéing with greens. Pour the bright pink vinegar into a clean narrow-mouth glass bottle with a cork or lid for storage and use. The vinegar will keep tightly sealed in the refrigerator for up to 6 months.

VANILLA VINEGAR
MAKES 1 PINT

1 vanilla bean (see Tip)

1 pint homemade apple cider vinegar (page 27) or red wine vinegar (page 27), or store-bought

1. Slice the bean lengthwise and place it and the vinegar in a clean pint-sized mason jar with a tight-fitting lid. Shake daily for at least 2 weeks, though it's even better after 4 weeks.

2. Remove the bean, scrape out the seeds, and return them to the jar. Pour the vinegar into a clean narrow-mouth glass bottle with a cork or lid for storage and use. The vinegar will keep tightly sealed in the refrigerator for up to 6 months.

TIP: Make sure you choose a vanilla bean that is still supple; you don't want something that has dried out to the point of breaking when you bend it because the flavor will be diminished and it will be harder to infuse.

CINNAMON APPLE CIDER SHRUB

MAKES ABOUT 1½ PINTS

This recipe for a fruit-based sugar syrup utilizes both the unfermented sweet cider and the product of the fermentation for a really tart, warm-spiced shrub. Rum is the best thing to mix with this, or make a refreshing spritzer with 2 ounces of shrub, a few ounces of Lillet, and a splash of seltzer.

2 cups fresh apple cider (the fresher, the better)

½ cup sugar

1½ cups homemade apple cider vinegar (page 27), or store-bought

1 (3-inch) cinnamon stick

½ teaspoon ground ginger

¼ teaspoon freshly grated nutmeg

1. In a small nonreactive saucepan, mix the cider with the sugar and vinegar. Stir in the cinnamon stick, ginger, and nutmeg.

2. Heat to a simmer over medium heat and then pour the entire mixture into a clean quart-sized mason jar with a tight-fitting lid, seal the jar, and refrigerate for 3 days.

3. Strain out the solids, discard, and use the shrub immediately. It will keep tightly sealed in the refrigerator for up to 6 months.

BLUEBERRY SHRUB

MAKES ABOUT 1½ PINTS

Antioxidants, summer breezes, and lip stains . . . this shrub yields an awesome color and packs a punch of goodness into your glass. I love stirring this shrub into lemonade and/or vodka. You can use frozen blueberries instead of fresh. Use sherry vinegar, which adds complexity to the blueberry. Sophisticated and bittersweet, this is more like *amaro*, the Italian herbal liqueur, than a soda.

2 cups fresh or frozen blueberries (there is no need to thaw them if you're using frozen)

1 cup sugar

2 cups store-bought sherry vinegar

½ teaspoon freshly grated nutmeg

TIP

While you can just add a dash of vinegar or shrub to straight alcohol to make a quick cocktail, consider using them as substitutes in your favorite recipes for classic cocktails: Use shrubs instead of juice, and vinegars or infusions in place of bitters or citrus. It's much easier to stock your home bar with one or two vinegars than multiple varieties of citrus and juice.

1. Place the berries and the sugar in a clean quart-sized mason jar with a tight-fitting lid and use a wooden spoon to crush the berries and macerate the flavors. Let the closed jar sit for 4 hours at room temperature.

2. In a small nonreactive saucepan over medium heat, heat the vinegar to just below boiling (about 200°F), then pour it over the blueberries and sugar. Add the nutmeg, seal the jar, and refrigerate overnight or up to 3 days.

3. Strain out the skins, discard, and use the shrub immediately. It will keep tightly sealed in the refrigerator for up to 6 months.

CRANBERRY SHRUB

MAKES ABOUT 1½ PINTS

This shrub is very tart and best made from fresh or frozen whole cranberries. You can substitute unsweetened cranberry juice instead—if you can find it. (The major brand varieties of juice almost always contain sugar and other preservatives.) I like to keep the sugar to a minimum in this one, but you can always dial it up. Add a little to your family cranberry sauce recipe at Thanksgiving; it's also a nice addition to a hot toddy.

4 cups whole cranberries (thawed if frozen) or 2 cups unsweetened cranberry juice

½ cup packed light brown sugar

1½ cups homemade apple cider vinegar (page 27), or store-bought

1 star anise

2 allspice berries

2 whole cloves

1. In a blender or food processor, pulse the cranberries until well chopped. (If you're using juice, skip this step.)

2. In a small nonreactive saucepan, combine the puree, sugar, vinegar, star anise, allspice, and cloves. Heat over medium heat to just below boiling (about 200°F) to blend the flavors.

3. Pour the mixture into a clean quart-sized mason jar with a tight-fitting lid, seal the jar, and refrigerate for 3 days.

4. Strain out the solids, discard, and use the shrub immediately. It will keep tightly sealed in the refrigerator for up to 6 months.

STRAWBERRY RHUBARB SHRUB

MAKES ABOUT 1 PINT

This recipe reminds me of my mother, whose favorite pie was strawberry rhubarb. This shrub is a little different because you have to cook the rhubarb and strawberries (like you're making jam) before adding the vinegar and letting it rest. Serve with gin, seltzer, and a dash of bitters for a cocktail that tastes like spring in a glass.

1 cup hulled, sliced strawberries

1 cup rhubarb cut into ½-inch pieces

1 teaspoon kosher salt

1 cup sugar

1½ cups homemade white wine vinegar (page 27), or store-bought

1. In a small nonreactive saucepan, mix the strawberries and rhubarb with the salt and sugar. Cook the mixture over medium heat, stirring frequently, until the fruit breaks down, about 5 minutes.

2. Add the vinegar, stir, and remove from the heat. Pour the mixture into a clean quart-sized mason jar with a tight-fitting lid, seal the jar, and refrigerate overnight.

3. Strain out the solids and use the shrub immediately. (The solids make a great sweet-tart addition to a bowl of granola and yogurt.) The shrub will keep tightly sealed in the refrigerator for up to 6 months.

CARROT GINGER SHRUB

MAKES ABOUT 1 PINT

This one is delicious added to a Bloody Mary; one ounce per cocktail will do the trick. It also makes a great brunch kir royale–style cocktail with prosecco or champagne.

1 cup unsweetened fresh carrot juice

1 cup sugar

2 tablespoons grated fresh ginger

1 cup homemade apple cider vinegar (page 27), or store-bought

1. In a medium nonreactive saucepan, combine the carrot juice and sugar. Heat over medium heat, bringing the liquid to a simmer to dissolve the sugar and reduce the liquid by a third, about 15 minutes. Remove from heat.

2. Add the ginger and vinegar, stir, and pour the mixture into a clean quart-sized mason jar with a tight-fitting lid, seal the jar, and refrigerate for 3 days.

3. Strain out and discard the ginger and use the shrub immediately. The shrub will keep tightly sealed in the refrigerator for up to 6 months. Shake before using.

LEMONGRASS HONEY SHRUB (PAGE 48)

LEMONGRASS HONEY SHRUB

MAKES ABOUT 1 PINT

Brush this on grilled pork or add to vodka and seltzer for a boost on a hot
August afternoon. Start this shrub at least a week before you want it—the
lemongrass needs some time to sit in the fridge before you even add the
vinegar.

½ cup thinly sliced lemongrass
(white parts only; see Tip)

½ cup honey

1½ cups store-bought distilled
white vinegar or homemade
rice (sake) vinegar (page 27), or
store-bought

TIP

To prepare lemongrass, peel
away the dried stringy outer
leaves and use the lighter and
fresher inside stalk. (Save the
dried parts and put them in
tea.) Lemongrass grows well
indoors; I keep a small plant in
my living room.

1. Using the back of a knife or a mortar
and pestle, bruise the lemongrass to
release its flavors. Place it and the honey
in a clean quart-sized mason jar with
a tight-fitting lid, seal the jar, and
refrigerate for 3 to 4 days.

2. In a small nonreactive saucepan
over medium heat, heat the vinegar to
a simmer (190°F) and pour it over the
lemongrass-honey mixture. Return the
jar to the refrigerator to infuse for at least
48 hours or up to 2 weeks.

3. Strain out and discard the solids.
Use the shrub immediately. It will keep
tightly sealed in the refrigerator for up
to 6 months.

MINT SHRUB

MAKES ABOUT 1 PINT

This is the base for the Mint Vinegar Julep (page 60), but add it to iced tea for an extra kick. Mint is so delicate that you don't need to cook it in order to capture the flavor, which is why you don't heat the vinegar in this shrub. The hot water will dissolve the sugar.

½ cup packed fresh mint leaves

½ cup sugar

½ cup hot (but not boiling) water

2 cups homemade apple cider vinegar (page 27), or store-bought

1. Place the mint and sugar in a clean quart-sized mason jar with a tight-fitting lid and muddle the mixture with a wooden spoon to bruise the leaves.

2. Add the hot water to dissolve the sugar, then fill the jar with the vinegar. Seal the jar and infuse the shrub in the refrigerator overnight or for up to 48 hours.

3. Strain out and discard the solids. Use the shrub immediately. It will keep tightly sealed in the refrigerator for up to 2 months.

ROSEMARY MAPLE SHRUB

MAKES ABOUT 1½ PINTS

This base is great for a soda that's best enjoyed with a view of fields (preferably the Italian hillside) or the ocean on a crisp fall day. Just mix 1 ounce of shrub with 10 ounces of seltzer and garnish with lemon. Stir in bourbon for a warming effect.

⅓ cup fresh rosemary leaves

1 tablespoon sugar

¾ cup good-quality maple syrup

2 cups homemade apple cider vinegar (page 27), or store-bought

1. Place the rosemary and sugar in a clean quart-sized mason jar with a tight-fitting lid. Muddle the rosemary and sugar with a wooden spoon to bruise the leaves and release the oils. Pour the maple syrup over the leaves, seal the jar, and infuse it in the refrigerator for 2 days.

2. Heat the apple cider vinegar in a nonreactive saucepan over medium heat to just below a boil (200°F) and add it to the jar.

3. Return the jar to the refrigerator to infuse for a week. Give it a good shake when you notice it in the fridge while you're looking for a midnight snack.

4. Strain out and discard the solids. Use the shrub immediately. It will keep tightly sealed in the refrigerator for up to 3 months.

DRINKS
AND
COCKTAILS

Acid adds the brightness that we've come to enjoy in just about every soda and juice. But more often than not, what you're tasting is citric acid, not acetic acid. Citric acid does two things: it preserves the beverage, and it lends the signature pucker that we now associate with "refreshment," thanks to decades of clever advertising. (Quite the contrary, however: we now know that soda does little to hydrate us but instead gives us a short-lived sugar high.) If you want something truly invigorating, try the recipes in this chapter, or just pour yourself a cold glass of seltzer, then splash an ounce of vinegar into it. Drink up!

FIERY CIDER

MAKES 1 QUART

This tonic is a traditional New England cure-all for lots of ailments, including aches and pains, colds, flu, congestion, and heartburn. Slug it first thing on those cold dark mornings in winter—its spicy punch will clear your nasal passages and wake you right up. You can also use it as a condiment like you would a hot sauce, or in sweet or savory cocktails. If you really like this stuff, this recipe scales well, and you can make it by the gallon.

4 tablespoons freshly grated or prepared horseradish

2 whole heads of garlic, cloves separated and smashed

½ cup chopped onion

1 cup chopped fresh ginger (see Tip)

3 fresh Thai chiles

1 teaspoon whole black peppercorns

¼ cup whole mint leaves

¼ cup whole parsley leaves

1 tablespoon whole rosemary leaves

1 tablespoon whole thyme leaves

1 tarragon sprig

Juice and pulp of 1 lemon

1 quart raw homemade apple cider vinegar (page 27), or store-bought

½ teaspoon ground ginger

½ teaspoon ground turmeric

¼ cup good quality maple syrup or honey, plus more as needed

1. In a clean half gallon–sized mason jar with a tight-fitting lid, mix together the horseradish, garlic, onion, fresh ginger, chiles, peppercorns, mint, parsley, rosemary, thyme, tarragon, and lemon juice and pulp. Pour in the cider vinegar to cover the ingredients and seal the jar.

2. Store the sealed jar at room temperature but out of direct sunlight. Shake the jar well once a day for 3 to 6 weeks.

3. Strain out and discard the solids; mix in the ground ginger, ground turmeric, and the maple syrup to taste. Fiery cider will keep tightly sealed in the refrigerator for up to 6 months. Shake before use.

TIP

Fresh herbs are preferable for this recipe and Four Thieves Vinegar (page 55), but dried will work if that's all you have. Cut the amounts in half for dried herbs.

VINEGAR THROUGH THE AGES

Vinegar is one of the oldest chemicals used by humans. Likely first "discovered" and cultured by the Egyptians and the Chinese, whether by accident or not, it is one of a host of products produced by bacteria that we now rely on. Consumed since biblical times as an energizing drink, and as medicine by Hippocrates, who prescribed it with honey as a remedy for coughs and colds, in recent years vinegar has been lauded more and more for its medicinal properties. Fiery Cider (page 53) is a classic New England health tonic made to keep winter colds and summer allergies at bay. For a great morning pick-me-up, take a shot of it—or just straight vinegar.

As a food preservative, vinegar is unmatched in usefulness, except perhaps by salt and the modern freezer. There is no question that the success of the human species is tied to vinegar, as it has allowed humankind the ability to keep food from rotting. I believe that without it, the population growth necessary to expand humanity worldwide would likely have been impossible, as we could never have moved away from warmer climates where cultivation is possible most of the year. Even cultures along the equator use vinegar to prevent meat from spoiling in the heat and humidity. Salt and vinegar work in concert for nearly bulletproof preservation and are the basis for pickling fruits and vegetables and delicious dishes like Roast Chicken Adobo (page 124).

Vinegar was used to cool cannons by Louis XIII, to break boulders by Hannibal during his famous crossing of the Alps, to provide strength and focus when consumed by samurai before battle, and to disinfect wounds on the battlefield as late as World War I. Cleopatra is purported to have won a bet with Marc Antony that she could eat a fortune in a single meal; to do so, she dissolved a pearl in a glass of vinegar and drank it for dessert.

FOUR THIEVES VINEGAR

MAKES 1 QUART

Legend has it that this brew originated around Marseille in the fourteenth century as a way to ward off the Black Death. Villagers would soak a scarf in the liquid and wear it around their mouths and noses. The concoction got its name from the famed "four thieves," who purportedly used the vinegar to stay disease-free while they plundered France and its dying masses. This recipe has hundreds of variations, so feel free to experiment and use whatever fresh and dried herbs you have on hand. Use topically as a bug repellent, or add 1 tablespoon to a glass of water at the first signs of plague.

2 tablespoons chopped fresh thyme (see Tip, page 53)

2 tablespoons chopped fresh rosemary

2 tablespoons chopped fresh sage

2 tablespoons chopped fresh lavender

2 tablespoons chopped fresh mint

6 garlic cloves, minced

1 teaspoon whole black peppercorns

1 quart raw homemade apple cider or wine vinegar (page 27), or store-bought

1. In a clean quart-sized mason jar or bottle with a tight-fitting lid, mix together the thyme, rosemary, sage, lavender, mint, garlic, and black peppercorns. Pour in the cider vinegar to cover the ingredients and seal the jar.

2. Store the sealed jar at room temperature but out of direct sunlight. Shake the jar well once a day for 3 to 6 weeks.

3. Strain out and discard the solids. This vinegar will keep tightly sealed in the refrigerator for up to 6 months.

SWITCHEL

MAKES 1 QUART

This old-fashioned energy drink is as colonial as it sounds. It's made from apple cider vinegar and New England's liquid gold, maple syrup. I find this to be the most refreshing thing you can slug on a hot summer day after working in the garden, changing the oil, or just sitting on the porch. Try it with a shot of bourbon at cocktail hour. You can triple or quadruple this recipe for a party—or just so you always have switchel close at hand.

½ cup homemade apple cider vinegar (page 27), or store-bought

3 tablespoons good-quality maple syrup

1 tablespoon grated fresh ginger or 2 teaspoons ground ginger

Pinch of kosher salt

½ lemon

1. In a clean quart-sized mason jar with a tight-fitting lid, mix together the vinegar, maple syrup, ginger, and salt. Squeeze the lemon juice into the jar and add the lemon half. Fill with water, seal the jar, and refrigerate for at least 4 hours.

2. Remove and discard the lemon; shake, drink, and enjoy. Switchel will keep tightly sealed in the refrigerator for up to 1 month (if you can make it last that long).

BY THE BOOK

In *The Long Winter* Laura Ingalls Wilder writes about the drink her mother made for them while they cut hay in the hot late summer of 1880, which sounds a lot like switchel. She described it as ginger water, sweetened with sugar and made tangy with vinegar. The ginger calmed their stomachs and allowed them to rehydrate, whereas plain water would've made them sick. Some old remedies still have merit!

VINEGAR MANHATTAN

MAKES 2 DRINKS

My perfect Manhattan is one part sweet vermouth, one part dry vermouth, and two parts rye whiskey with a dash of bitters—cherry optional. Skipping the bitters in favor of adding one part vinegar turns this into more of a pick-me-up than a dark sipper. I like a hint of sweetness so I drop in a cherry. This drink can be mixed in a large batch and served at a party. If it's summer, serve it with one or two rocks.

3 ounces rye whiskey

1½ ounces sweet vermouth

1½ ounces dry vermouth

1½ ounces homemade apple cider vinegar (page 27) or Honey Vinegar (page 31), or store-bought

1 cup crushed ice

2 to 4 maraschino cherries (preferably Luxardo; optional)

1. Into a cocktail shaker, pour the whiskey, vermouth, and vinegar over ice. Shake or stir (your choice, 007), then strain, discarding the solids and evenly dividing the liquid among 2 coupe glasses.

2. Garnish each drink with a cherry or two, if desired. Look each other in the eye, clink glasses, and sip.

VINEGAR SHANDY

MAKES 1 LARGE PITCHER (ABOUT 64 OUNCES)

Shandies are usually a lemonade and beer mash-up best enjoyed in summer. Since you're watering down the beer, you can really throw them back. Mix Lemongrass Honey Shrub (page 48) with a cool, crisp lager to brighten up your summer barbecue.

1 cup shrub of your choice (see pages 40–50)

3 cups crushed ice

4 (12-ounce) bottles light lager beer, chilled

In a large pitcher, pour the shrub over the ice. Add the beer and stir a few times to mix well. Serve in chilled glasses.

MINT VINEGAR JULEP

MAKES 4 DRINKS

The official drink of the Kentucky Derby, a julep made with extra acid will help keep your senses keen when choosing the winning stead. If you happen to have crushed ice and julep cups ready for race day, then by all means use them, but this is fine in a regular cup on a Tuesday over (gasp) regular ice cubes.

2 to 3 cups crushed ice

12 ounces bourbon

4 ounces Mint Shrub
(page 49)

4 fresh mint sprigs

1. Fill 4 glasses or julep cups halfway with crushed ice.

2. Mix the bourbon and the shrub in a cocktail shaker. Divide the liquid evenly among 4 glasses or julep cups.

3. Fill the glasses the rest of the way with crushed ice. Garnish with a sprig of fresh mint and bet on the horse with the best name.

DIRTY VINEGAR MARTINI

MAKES 2 DRINKS

I like a martini that's about 110 percent cold gin with just a whisper of olive juice. This version is slightly more savory than my old standby, with some pickle juice and pickles for garnish. I love tossing in the brine and pickles from the Pickled Fennel (page 70); the Dill Pickles (page 69) works well for this, too.

6 ounces gin (such as New York Distilling Company's Dorothy Parker, though Tanqueray is great, too)

1 ounce pickle brine

1 cup crushed ice

2 pickle slices, for garnish

Mix the gin and pickle brine in a cocktail shaker and add the ice. Shake or stir to combine and strain into 2 martini or coupe glasses. Garnish with the pickles and serve immediately.

GIN AND VINEGAR FIZZ

MAKES 2 DRINKS

If you want the full fizz experience, shake this drink hard for two minutes with the egg white before adding ice and shaking it a little more. If you're squeamish about consuming raw egg and can't find pasteurized eggs, then you can omit it, shake briefly, and enjoy; however, you won't achieve the same great texture.

3 ounces gin

3 ounces Cranberry Shrub (page 43) or any other shrub you like

1 ounce egg white (see Tip)

1 cup crushed ice

2 to 3 ounces seltzer

Mix the gin, shrub, and egg white in a shaker and shake hard for 1 to 2 minutes. Add the ice and shake for another 20 seconds. Strain into a highball glass and top with seltzer.

TIP

A typical egg white is about 1.5 fluid ounces, so you'll want to measure out less than that or just use 2 eggs and triple the recipe.

PICKLES AND PRESERVES

Clearly this is the most obvious application for vinegar and the one that we go to first when vinegar comes up in conversation. Pickling with your own vinegars opens up all kinds of flavorful doors, and you should feel free to use any homemade vinegar for the pickle recipes that follow. Think about what your rice vinegar will do to the whole garlic (page 81), or malt vinegar with fennel (page 70)—yum! To gift them or keep them for longer pantry storage, feel free to can any of the vegetable recipes in a water bath; it's easier than you think. All the recipes in this chapter are based on smaller amounts that yield a few jars at a time. If you want to do a whole run of something and stock up for winter, you can multiply the recipes as desired.

CRUCIAL NOTE: DO NOT use your homemade vinegar for canning pickles to make them shelf stable. You must use vinegar that has at least 5 percent acidity. Also, for shelf-stable storage of any pickling recipes with protein (meat, fish, or eggs) they must be canned in a pressure canner, which is not covered in this book.

COCKTAIL ONIONS
AND CORNICHONS

MAKES 2 (8-OUNCE) JARS

These small pickles are great on a cheese plate, with mustard and pretzels, and as garnishes for martinis. Kids seem to love them, as the tiny cucumbers always make them feel like giants. The trick here is finding the cornichons. They're hard to grow and harvest, so talk to your local farmers to see if and when they'll be available and plan ahead. These do well in 8-ounce jars as the vegetables are small.

2 fresh pearl onions (see Tips)

24 cornichon cucumbers, flowering end trimmed (see Tips)

2 tablespoons kosher salt

2 tarragon sprigs

1 cup homemade white wine vinegar (page 27), or store-bought

TIPS

To save time and trouble, look for frozen pearl onions, which have already been blanched and peeled, or substitute onion or shallot wedges—just skip step 1.

If you can't find cornichons, you can use ½-inch slices of any thin-skinned cucumber.

1. Prepare an ice bath and bring a small nonreactive saucepan of water to a boil over medium high heat. Add the pearl onions to the pot and blanch for 4 minutes. Remove the onions to the ice bath; when the onions are cool, peel off the skins and discard.

2. In a medium nonreactive bowl, toss the onions and cornichons with salt, cover, and let them rest in the fridge overnight.

3. The next day, rinse the vegetables well in cold water, divide them, and pack them into 2 clean 8-ounce mason jars, with a sprig of tarragon in each. Mix ½ cup of water with the vinegar and pour the mixture into the jars, leaving ½ inch of headspace if canning. Screw on the lids and rings.

4. Either refrigerate the jars once they have cooled, or, while still hot, follow the steps on page 66 for water-bath canning to make them shelf stable, processing for 10 minutes. Whether fresh or canned, the pickles should rest for 5 to 7 days before you eat them. They will keep in a tightly sealed container in the refrigerator for up to 6 months.

The most basic vinegar pickle recipe includes a 1:1 ratio of vinegar to water; boil the liquid with some sugar, salt, and spices, then pour it over vegetables. Stick them in the fridge and taste them after a few days of sitting in the brine. Once you're ready to put up your pickles and make them shelf stable, then you'll want to can the jars using a water bath, which will give any unwanted microbes in your jar a one-two punch by lowering the pH level and pasteurizing the vegetables in hot water to help prevent botulism. Always use a trusted recipe when canning; for fridge pickles, feel free to experiment to your heart's desire.

If you want to can with homemade vinegar, you'll have to check the pH and the acid percentage (see page 150) to determine whether or not you have enough acid. Anything made with a vinegar with less than 5 percent acid should always be consumed as a quick pickle or stored in the refrigerator for up to two weeks. For pickling, you don't want to use shrubs or other vinegar infusions that have components and flavorings other than just vinegar, which could throw off your vinegar's pH and acid content. Remember that even a sprig of fresh herb contains water and other substances that will affect your final pH. Once processed, pickles and preserves keep on the shelf for one year.

HOW TO CAN

There are many types of canning jars out there; this book uses standard Ball mason jars with a flat lid and ring. You can reuse the glass jars and the ring that holds the lid on, but don't reuse the flat lids that come in contact with the food; buy new ones every time. If you choose another type of jar, follow that manufacturer's directions.

YOU WILL NEED THE FOLLOWING:

Large stockpot or canning pot

Jar lifter

Jars

Canning rack (or you can use a clean towel at the bottom of your stockpot to keep the jars from rattling)

Lid lifter or tongs

Unused lids and rings

Canning funnel (optional)

1. Fill a stockpot two-thirds full with water and bring the water to a boil. Prep your ingredients and make your brine. Keep the brine at a simmer.

2. Once the stockpot has reached a boil, use the jar lifter to place the empty jars in the boiling water for 5 minutes to sterilize them. Pour out any water and remove them to a clean towel or rack, right side up (keep the lip of the jar from coming into contact with anything other than the lid). Place the lids in a glass bowl and use a ladle to cover them with boiling water. Keep the water at a boil.

3. Add your preferred vegetables and any spices to the jars and then pour in the hot vinegar brine. Make sure to leave the proper amount of head-space: ¼ inch for 8-ounce jars and ½ inch for pint- and quart-sized jars. Place a lid and ring on the jar and then screw down the lid using only your thumb and first two fingers. You want a tight seal without overtighten-ing the ring.

4. Using the jar lifter, return the full jars to the boiling water in the stockpot. Process the jars for the amount of time specified in the recipe. Remove the jars to a towel or rack on the counter; don't put a hot jar directly onto a cold counter like granite or marble, as it may fracture from the temperature shock.

5. Once the jars are completely cool, check that the lids are all concave. You can test your seals by removing the rings and lifting the jars only by their lids. You should be able to lift the whole jar by the lid without it coming off.

6. If any lids are popped up, check that the jars have enough headspace, make sure the rims are clean, and reprocess them immediately, or keep them in the fridge and use them within 2 weeks.

DILL PICKLES

MAKES 1 QUART

When I met Bob McClure in 2006, he had just started McClure's pickles with his brother Joe. At the Brooklyn Kitchen, we were the first store to carry their product. Based on their great-grandmother's spicy dill pickle recipe, these remain one of my favorite pickles on a sandwich, minced in tuna or egg salad, or as an anytime snack. Bright and crunchy with fresh dill fronds (if you can get them) and whole cloves of garlic, these pickles are so good that you might just eat the whole jar in one go. They also make a great addition to a Bloody Mary—and don't forget to add the brine to your drink for some extra sour.

1½ tablespoons kosher salt

2 cups store-bought distilled white vinegar

5 to 6 Kirby cucumbers or other small cucumbers, sliced lengthwise into fourths (see Tip)

2 garlic cloves, split in half lengthwise

1 flowering or fresh dill sprig or ½ teaspoon dried dill

½ teaspoon whole black peppercorns

½ teaspoon coriander seed

¼ teaspoon celery seed

TIP

Cut the blossom ends off the cucumbers to keep the pickles extra crispy.

1. Combine the salt, vinegar, and 1 cup of water in a medium nonreactive saucepan and bring to a boil over medium high heat, stirring continuously until the salt has dissolved. Once it reaches a boil, turn the heat to low and simmer for 2 minutes.

2. Meanwhile, pack a clean quart-sized mason jar with the garlic, dill, peppercorns, coriander, and celery seed. Add the cucumbers (depending on the cukes you're using, they may not all fit). Pour the hot brine over the ingredients, make sure to leave ½ inch of headspace if canning, and screw on a lid and ring.

3. Either refrigerate the jar once it has cooled, or, to make it shelf stable, follow the steps on page 66 for water-bath canning while still hot, processing for 15 minutes. Whether fresh or canned, the pickles should rest for 7 to 10 days before you eat them. They will keep in a tightly sealed container in the refrigerator for up to 6 months.

PICKLED FENNEL WITH CARDAMOM

MAKES 1 PINT

This is what I would call a dinner pickle; it's a sophisticated preserve perfect for rice bowls (see page 133). Make sure to cut the fennel at a consistent thickness (ideally on a mandoline) so the slices pickle at the same rate, and rinse the fennel well, as it can be sandy.

1 fennel bulb, cut into ¼-inch slices, frond(s) reserved (see Tip)

1 tablespoon kosher salt

4 green cardamom pods

½ teaspoon yellow mustard seed

½ teaspoon crushed red pepper flakes

1 cup homemade white wine vinegar (page 27) or apple cider vinegar (page 27), or store-bought

1 tablespoon sugar

1 garlic clove, peeled and smashed

TIP

Carrots and beets sliced into ¼-inch batons can be substituted for the fennel.

1. In a medium bowl, toss together the fennel and salt; set the mixture aside while you prepare the brine.

2. In a small nonreactive saucepan, toast the cardamom pods and mustard seed over low heat until fragrant, about 1 minute, then add the pepper flakes. Add the vinegar, sugar, and 1½ cup of water, and bring to a boil over tk heat; immediately remove the pan from the heat.

3. Place the garlic clove at the bottom of a clean pint-sized mason jar, then pack the fennel on top with a 3-inch piece of fennel frond. Pour the hot liquid over the vegetables, leaving ½ inch of headspace if canning, and screw on the lid and ring.

4. Either refrigerate the jar once it has cooled, or, while still hot, follow the steps on page 66 for water-bath canning to make it shelf stable, processing for 10 minutes. Whether fresh or canned, the pickles should rest for 7 to 10 days before you eat them. They will keep in a tightly sealed container in the refrigerator for up to 6 months.

PICKLED BEETS

MAKES 1 QUART

Choose only red beets if you also want to make pink Pickled Eggs (opposite page); otherwise you can use any variety, including Chiogga or golden. One thing to remember about making beet pickles is that you want them a little crunchy—so cook them a bit less than you would if preparing them to eat hot. These make a great addition to egg salad or accompaniment to charcuterie.

1½ pounds beets

2 cups homemade red wine vinegar (page 27), or store-bought distilled white vinegar

1 teaspoon kosher salt

3 garlic cloves

1 tablespoon coriander seed

1 tablespoon cumin seed, toasted

1 (1-inch) cinnamon stick

TIP

Once you've eaten all of the beets, save the brine for making Pickled Eggs (opposite page).

1. Fill a large nonreactive saucepan three-quarters full with water and bring it to a boil over high heat. Meanwhile, peel and cut the beets into ¾-inch cubes. Add the beets to the water and boil for 5 minutes. Drain the beets, reserving 1 cup of the cooking liquid.

2. Return the reserved cooking liquid to the saucepan and add the vinegar and salt. Bring to a simmer over medium heat. Pack the beets into a clean quart-sized mason jar and add the garlic, coriander, cumin, and cinnamon stick. Pour the hot liquid over the beets and screw on a lid and ring.

3. Either refrigerate the jar once it has cooled, or, while still hot, follow the steps on page 66 for water-bath canning to make it shelf stable, processing for 20 minutes. Whether fresh or canned, the pickles should rest for 5 to 7 days before you eat them. They will keep in a tightly sealed container in the refrigerator for up to 6 months.

PICKLED EGGS

MAKES 8 EGGS

Sometimes I wish I lived in the days when all bars and saloons kept pickled eggs on the counter. These and other pickled foods—along with bread, cheese, and onions—were the food of nineteenth-century laborers, and as long as they were buying drinks, they could eat for free. These eggs are bright red and taste like the pickled beets they borrow their brine from. You can make this without the beet brine (though you'll miss the color); just use the brine on the opposite page and add the eggs instead of the beets. Slice these eggs in half before eating for the fullest expression of color contrast between the now pink whites and the bright yellow yolks.

8 large eggs

Brine from Pickled Beets (opposite page)

TIP

If you plan to use these pickled eggs to make deviled eggs (page 103) remove them from the brine after 3 days so that they maintain the best color. (Eventually the whole yolk will turn pink from sitting in the vinegar.)

1. Prepare an ice bath. Place the eggs in a saucepan, add cold water to cover, and bring to a boil over high heat. As soon as the water boils, remove the pan from the heat, and cover. Let the eggs sit for 12 minutes.

2. Drain and transfer them to a bowl of ice water to stop them from cooking further.

3. When the eggs are cool enough to handle, peel them and place them in a quart-sized mason jar with the bright red brine, and screw on a lid and ring. Refrigerate for at least 3 days to allow the flavor and color to permeate the eggs. The eggs will keep in a tightly sealed container in the refrigerator for up to 1 month.

NATURALLY DYED EASTER EGGS

I have a clear memory from my childhood of the smell of distilled white vinegar wafting through the house when we dyed Easter eggs. You can make natural dyes from vegetable scraps and spices like turmeric that yield less neon and more traditional-looking colors, albeit still bright and deeply hued. The acid helps the dye to penetrate the shell.

THE BASIC METHOD IS AS FOLLOWS:

1. Choose a vegetable or spice for the dye, for example, onion skins (red or yellow), red cabbage, spinach, blueberries, chili powder, or beets.

2. To a 3-quart saucepan, add 1 cup of vegetable for every cup of water, or 2 tablespoons of dried spice for every cup of water.

3. Bring to a simmer, cover, and cook for 30 minutes.

4. Cool the liquid, strain out any solids, and add distilled white vinegar to the water in a ratio of ½ cup of vinegar for every quart of dye.

5. Immerse your boiled eggs in the dye for a few hours or up to 2 days, storing them in a covered container in the refrigerator, until you achieve your desired shade.

QUICK PICKLED CARROTS
AND GINGER

Choose carrots and knobs of ginger that are about the same circumference so that when you shave them (super thin, almost see-through), they are quickly pickled and you can add a pile to your sushi plate. You can also eat them as a palate cleanser with pâté or any heavy organ meat.

4 medium carrots

1 Fuji (or other very crisp) apple, cored and quartered

3- to 4-inch knob of fresh ginger, peeled

½ cup mirin

1 cup homemade rice (sake) vinegar (page 27), or store-bought

2 tablespoons coriander seed

1. Shave the carrots, apple, and ginger crosswise as thinly as possible on a mandoline or with a chef's knife, then place them in a medium bowl and stir to combine. You want them to be small rounds of carrot and ginger that are about the same size as the slices of apple.

2. In a small nonreactive bowl, whisk together the mirin and vinegar and set it aside. Pack the carrot, apple, and ginger slices into a clean pint-sized mason jar with a tight-fitting lid, or place them in a medium nonreactive bowl.

3. Sprinkle coriander over the slices and add the vinegar-mirin mixture.

4. Enjoy the quick pickles immediately. The pickles will keep in a tightly sealed container in the refrigerator for up to 1 month.

PICKLED JALAPEÑOS

MAKES 1 PINT

This is a great addition to a pickle plate, chili, corn bread, or a rice bowl. I always create these pickles for our annual New Year's Day chili party, which is just the thing to follow the long night most people had the evening before. I like to pickle these in the fridge, as they stay crunchier than if you preserve them in a water bath, but you can pour the vinegar over them hot and process them for shelf stability if you'd like.

1 cup homemade apple cider vinegar (page 27), or store-bought

½ cup good-quality maple syrup

Pinch of kosher salt

8 jalapeños, seeded and sliced lengthwise into thirds (see Tip)

TIP

Wear gloves while seeding and slicing the jalapeños to prevent the volatile oils from sticking to your skin and burning it.

1. In a small nonreactive saucepan over medium high heat, heat the vinegar, maple syrup, ½ cup of water, and salt just until boiling. Remove the pan from the heat and let it cool for about 30 minutes.

2. Wearing gloves, pack the jalapeños into a clean pint-sized mason jar with a tight-fitting lid.

3. Once the brine is cool, pour the mixture over the jalapeños, seal the jar, and refrigerate for a day or so before enjoying, or follow the steps on page 66 for water-bath canning to make it shelf stable, processing for 10 minutes. The pickles will keep in a tightly sealed container in the refrigerator for up to 3 months.

PICKLED WHOLE GARLIC (PAGE 81)

PICKLED PEPPERS (PAGE 36)

DILL PICKLES (PAGE 69)

PICKLED JALAPEÑOS (PAGE 77)

QUICK PICKLED CARROTS
AND GINGER (PAGE 76)

CURED GRAPES (PAGE 84)

PICKLED FENNEL WITH CARDAMOM (PAGE 70)

PICKLED BEETS (PAGE 72)

PICKLED WHOLE GARLIC

MAKES 6 HEADS OF GARLIC

This recipe might become your new secret weapon in the kitchen: slice and sauté the garlic cloves with greens, add them whole or mashed to your soup, or slice them thin, mix with bread crumbs, and sprinkle on fish before it hits the broiler. The tart richness will add depth to all these dishes and more. Peeling enough garlic cloves to fill a jar is a ton of work; whole heads look way cooler in the jar and on the table anyway. This recipe also works well in the spring with early garlic if you can get it.

2 teaspoons coriander seed

3 cups homemade apple cider vinegar (page 27), or store-bought

4 tablespoons sugar

1 teaspoon whole black peppercorns

2 small dried chiles, such as arbol or Thai chiles

1 bay leaf

Two ½-inch by 2-inch slices of lemon peel

6 heads of garlic, outermost layers removed (see Tip)

1. In a small skillet, toast the coriander seed over medium heat until fragrant; set aside.

2. In a medium nonreactive saucepan, combine the vinegar, 1 cup of water, sugar, peppercorns, chiles, bay leaf, lemon peel, and toasted coriander. Bring the liquid to a boil over high heat. Add the garlic heads, reduce the heat to low, and simmer for 4 minutes.

3. Remove the heads of garlic, liquid, and spices from the saucepan, place them in a clean wide-mouth quart-sized mason jar, and screw on a lid and ring.

4. To make the garlic shelf stable, while the brine is still hot follow the steps on page 66 for water-bath canning, processing for 15 minutes. The garlic will keep in a tightly sealed container in the refrigerator for up to 3 months.

TIP

You can use this recipe for peeled garlic as well; just reduce the cooking time to 2 minutes, as the peeled cloves cook much faster than the whole heads.

PRESERVED CLAMS

MAKES ABOUT ½ PINT

This recipe was born during a vacation on the coast of Maine. We feasted on lobster and clams on the porch and threw the shells back into Penobscot Bay. Sometimes we ordered too many clams. I know, there's no such thing, but when you're crying uncle with a pound and a half left to go, you have to get creative. Pickling is a great way to save leftovers if you're not going to finish them, especially those that are prone to easy spoilage, like mollusks and shellfish. Once cold, the steamers just aren't as good, and if you're not in the mood to make chowder, then make these to serve on rice or as part of a spread of morsels for noshing.

1 cup cooked and cleaned soft-shell or steamer clams removed from the shells (see Tip)

½ cup homemade malt (beer) vinegar (page 27), or store-bought

1 tablespoon good-quality maple syrup

1 teaspoon toasted sesame oil

½ teaspoon crushed red pepper flakes

1. Place the cooked clams in a clean 8-ounce mason jar with a tight-fitting lid. In a small nonreactive bowl, whisk together the vinegar, maple syrup, sesame oil, and pepper flakes.

2. Pour the mixture over the clams, seal the jar, and store in the refrigerator. Wait at least 1 day before eating. The clams will keep in the refrigerator for up to 2 weeks.

TIP

Clean the clams by removing the two halves of the shell and the thick membrane that covers the neck. You should be left with the neck and belly.

PICKLED SMOKED PIG'S FEET

MAKES ABOUT 1 PINT

Nose-to-tail eating isn't a fad; it's the best way to get the most from an animal that has given its life so that we may eat. This recipe makes a delicious, unctuous, and (optionally) fiery addition to a picnic. You don't have to use smoked pig's feet; however, the smokiness and vinegar brine really make these taste great—not at all like you're eating feet—and the collagen gives them a great jellied texture. Add thinly sliced red and/or green chiles for a splash of spice and color in the jars. Serve with a strong mustard and dark bread.

2 smoked pig's feet or hocks (see Tip)

1 onion, quartered

2 cups homemade apple cider vinegar (page 27), or store-bought

1 jalapeño pepper or other fresh chile (optional)

TIP

Any good butcher should have smoked feet and hocks, or you can order them online.

1. Place the pig's feet, onion, and 2 quarts of water in a 3-quart saucepan or small stockpot and simmer for 2 to 3 hours, until the meat starts to fall off the bone. (Alternately you can pressure-cook the feet with half the water for 1 hour, following the manufacturer's directions.)

2. Remove the feet to a bowl to cool. Boil the remaining liquid to reduce by half and set aside. When the feet have cooled enough to handle, remove them to a cutting board, and carefully pick out all the bones (there are a lot of them). Separate the skin from the tendon and meat. If the feet don't have any hairs, then you can keep the skin; otherwise discard it.

3. Chop the meat, tissue, and skin into small pieces. Return the meat to the pot with the reserved broth, add the vinegar, and bring to a boil. Remove from the heat and add the jalapeño, if using.

4. Pack the meat and brine into a clean pint-sized mason jar or small terrine mold with a tight-fitting lid and refrigerate at least overnight to set. The pickled feet will keep in a tightly sealed container in the refrigerator for up to 1 month.

CURED GRAPES

MAKES ABOUT 1 QUART

One of the first products we made before we opened Brooklyn Kitchen was pickled grapes. When Taylor and I bought our house in Greenpoint, Brooklyn, in October 2004, there was a grapevine in the backyard. The next summer we had about thirty-five pounds of grapes that all ripened at the same time. It seemed like we had too few grapes to make wine, so we set out to eat as many as we could and preserve the rest. Small yellow or golden seedless grapes work best for this recipe, but any seedless variety will do. Bring these out for a cheese plate or as a topping for ice cream.

1½ cups homemade apple cider vinegar (page 27), or store bought

½ cup packed light brown sugar

6 slices of fresh ginger (each about the size of a quarter)

½ teaspoon whole black peppercorns

½ teaspoon kosher salt

1 (3-inch) cinnamon stick

1 bay leaf

1 pound seedless grapes, stems removed

1. Combine the vinegar, brown sugar, 1 cup of water, ginger, peppercorns, salt, cinnamon stick, and bay leaf in a nonreactive saucepan over medium heat, and simmer just long enough to dissolve the sugar and combine the flavors.

2. Place the grapes in a heatproof, non-reactive medium bowl and pour the hot brine over the grapes. Let stand until cool, about 30 minutes, then discard the cinnamon stick.

3. Pack the grapes and brine into a clean quart-sized mason jar and screw on a lid and ring. Refrigerate for at least 24 hours before enjoying, or follow the steps on page 66 for water-bath canning to make them shelf stable, packing them hot into 4 (8-ounce) mason jars and processing for 15 minutes. The grapes will keep in a tightly sealed container in the refrigerator for up to 2 months.

SAUCES, CONDIMENTS, AND VINAIGRETTES

Vinegar is the key ingredient that makes all condiments tick. Its importance as a preservative is paramount: not only does lowering the pH give us the tang we want in things like ketchup and mustard, but it also allows them to keep without refrigeration. When I was twelve, my father yelled from the kitchen for all of us to come see what he had discovered on the bottle of ketchup: the label said it did not need to be refrigerated. Space in the fridge was made available, and the Heinz bottle took up residence on the counter forever after.

MASTER VINAIGRETTE

MAKES ABOUT 1 PINT

Making a quick vinaigrette seems like a breeze, but sometimes you get the
ratio off, and it just doesn't work out. Memorize the basic vinegar-to-oil ratio
of 1:3 (some of these recipes stray a bit from that, but you can always tune your
vinaigrette to your tastes) and you'll be able to whip up a perfect dressing for
more than just salad—potatoes, roasted vegetables, chicken, tofu, and more.
Variations abound: add mustard, miso, or roasted garlic to help emulsify the oil,
and while fresh herbs are always best, dry herbs are fine. Don't forget the salt
and maybe a little sweetener if it needs it; maple syrup and honey are both good
options, though plain sugar works, too. See how versatile a good vinaigrette
can be?

½ cup homemade wine vinegar
of your choice (page 27), or
store-bought

3 tablespoons minced shallot

1 tablespoon Dijon mustard

1 teaspoon kosher salt

Freshly ground black pepper
to taste

1¼ cups extra-virgin olive oil
(see Tip)

While you can place everything except the
oil in a nonreactive bowl, and then slowly
whisk in the oil to emulsify it, I like to add
everything to a clean pint-sized mason
jar with a tight-fitting lid. Seal the jar and
shake like hell. The vinaigrette will keep
in a tightly sealed container in the refrigerator for up to 1 month.

TIP

I prefer olive oil, but you
can use any high-quality
cold-pressed oil, including
grapeseed or sunflower.

SMOKY GARLIC VINAIGRETTE

This vinaigrette is delicious on baked fish, especially pollack or cod.

½ cup homemade apple cider vinegar (page 27), or store-bought

3 tablespoons mashed roasted garlic

1 teaspoon liquid smoke (optional)

1 teaspoon kosher salt

Freshly ground black pepper to taste

1½ cups extra-virgin olive oil

CURRY VINAIGRETTE

I mix this incredibly versatile vinaigrette into chicken salad or pour it over grated carrot and parsnip slaw with raisins.

½ cup homemade apple cider vinegar (page 27), or store-bought

3 tablespoons minced shallot

1 tablespoon Dijon mustard

1 teaspoon curry powder

1 teaspoon kosher salt

1¼ cups extra-virgin olive oil

DASHI-SESAME VINAIGRETTE

Pour this sauce over cold ramen noodles for a quick dinner. This tastes great using white wine vinegar or rice vinegar, if you don't make the dashi one.

½ cup Dashi Vinegar (page 38), or store-bought

2 tablespoons minced scallions (white and green parts)

1 teaspoon toasted sesame oil

1 tablespoon tahini

1 teaspoon kosher salt

Freshly ground black pepper to taste

1 cup extra-virgin olive oil

SPICY VINAIGRETTE

This is a great quick marinade for chopped cucumbers.

½ cup homemade white wine vinegar (page 27), or store-bought

1 teaspoon Tabasco sauce

1 tablespoon good-quality maple syrup

1 teaspoon kosher salt

Freshly ground black pepper to taste

1 cup extra-virgin olive oil

MISO-GINGER VINAIGRETTE

Pour over roasted cauliflower or dress salmon with this before roasting it in the oven.

½ cup homemade rice (sake) vinegar (page 27), or store-bought

2 tablespoons white miso

1 tablespoon grated fresh ginger

1 teaspoon kosher salt

Freshly ground black pepper to taste

1½ cups extra-virgin olive oil

HERB VINAIGRETTE

This is an awesome all-purpose marinade for meats, and goes just as well on rice or quinoa. Simply grind all dry ingredients in a mortar and pestle before combining with the vinegar and oil. Season to taste with the black pepper.

1 teaspoon dried oregano

1 teaspoon dried rosemary

1 teaspoon dried thyme

1 teaspoon toasted cumin seed

1 teaspoon kosher salt

1 garlic clove

½ cup homemade cider or white wine vinegar (page 27), or store-bought

1¼ cups extra-virgin olive oil

Freshly ground black pepper to taste

SHERRY CAESAR VINAIGRETTE

Although lemon is a traditional ingredient in Caesar salad, at 7 percent acid, sherry vinegar makes a strong stand-in. You'll need to use a mortar and pestle to mash the anchovies, garlic, and salt.

6 anchovy fillets, drained

2 garlic cloves, minced

½ teaspoon kosher salt

2 egg yolks

1 teaspoon Dijon mustard

¼ cup store-bought sherry vinegar

½ cup extra-virgin olive oil

¼ cup freshly grated Parmesan cheese

Freshly ground black pepper to taste

YOGURT-PARSLEY VINAIGRETTE

Pour this over roasted sweet potatoes or a spinach salad.

½ cup homemade white wine vinegar (page 27), or store-bought

¼ cup finely minced fresh parsley

⅓ cup full-fat yogurt

1 teaspoon honey

½ teaspoon mustard powder, such as Coleman's

1 garlic clove, minced into a paste

½ teaspoon kosher salt

Freshly ground black pepper to taste

1¼ cups extra-virgin olive oil

SPICY KETCHUP
WITH SHICHIMI TOGARASHI

MAKES ABOUT 1 QUART

To me, there is nothing—and I mean nothing—that compares with Heinz ketchup, but this great condiment will stand up to spicy hot dogs, burgers, or those homemade fries you're determined to make even though you know the oil will turn your whole kitchen into a slick mess for days. The seasoning this recipe calls for is a Japanese blend. You can easily split this recipe in half.

8 pounds ripe tomatoes, coarsely chopped

1 large onion, finely chopped

2 cups homemade apple cider vinegar (page 27), or store-bought

3 tablespoons kosher salt

2 tablespoons granulated sugar

1 teaspoon shichimi togarashi (see Tip)

½ teaspoon ground fenugreek

1 tablespoon dark brown sugar

TIP

Look for *shichimi togarashi* online or at Asian groceries.

1. In a medium nonreactive stockpot, combine the tomatoes and onion and bring to a simmer over medium heat. Cook until the tomatoes and onions are soft, about 40 minutes.

2. Using a potato masher or wooden spoon, mash the tomatoes and onions in the pan, then strain them through a sieve or food mill to remove the tomato skins, seeds, and any other solids, pressing as much of the puree through as possible. You should have about 4 quarts of puree, depending on how juicy your tomatoes are.

3. Return the puree to the stockpot and add the vinegar, salt, granulated sugar, and shichimi togarashi. Bring to a simmer and cook, stirring every 15 minutes or so to prevent scorching, for about 2 hours or more, until the sauce is the consistency of ketchup.

4. Remove the stockpot from the heat and stir in the fenugreek and brown sugar. Pack the ketchup into a clean quart-sized mason jar and screw on a lid and ring. Store the ketchup in the fridge for up to 3 months.

REAL MUSTARD

MAKES ABOUT 1½ CUPS

Making your own mustard can take many forms: you can start from whole or ground seed, but make sure you use vinegar. I like to use whole seed, or you can blend the mustard for smoothness for better spreading. Interestingly enough, you can adjust the fieriness of your mustard by adjusting the temperature of the brine. It's an inverse proportion: cool the brine first for spicier mustard, or use hot brine for a milder flavor. This recipe halves well if you don't want to make so much.

½ cup homemade malt (beer) vinegar (page 27), or store-bought

½ cup brown ale or dark medium-bodied beer

1 teaspoon kosher salt

1 tablespoon light brown sugar

½ cup mustard seed (yellow, brown, or a mix)

1. In a small nonreactive saucepan, bring the vinegar, beer, salt, and sugar to a boil over medium-high heat. Remove from the heat and stir in the mustard seed (let the brine cool first for a hotter, spicier mustard). Pour the mixture into a clean pint-sized mason jar.

2. Allow the mustard to cool to room temperature, seal the jar, and then refrigerate for 2 to 3 days. Use as is, or blend in a mortar and pestle, food processor, or blender to your desired consistency. The mustard will keep in a tightly sealed container in the refrigerator for up to 3 months.

MUSTARD CAVIAR

MAKES ABOUT 1 CUP

I love mustard. It's a condiment that goes with just about everything and hits all the right buttons of zest and brightness with the addition of vinegar. I remember eating spicy mustard on steak in Provence when I was an exchange student, and now I can't have steak without good-quality mustard. This crunchy condiment pops in the mouth like caviar, hence its name. Serve it on rustic bread with ham and cheese, and use it in martinis, too.

½ cup homemade white wine vinegar (page 27), or store-bought

2 garlic cloves, coarsely chopped

1 (2-inch) thyme sprig

1 bay leaf

20 whole black peppercorns

½ cup yellow mustard seed (see Tip)

3 tablespoons bourbon or rum

1 tablespoon good-quality maple syrup or honey

½ teaspoon kosher salt

1. Combine the vinegar, 1 tablespoon of water, the garlic, thyme, bay leaf, and peppercorns in a small nonreactive saucepan and bring to a boil over medium-high heat. Remove the pan from the heat and set aside to cool and infuse the flavors.

2. Combine the mustard seed and bourbon in a small nonreactive bowl. Strain the vinegar mixture into the bowl, cover, and let stand at room temperature overnight.

3. Stir in the maple syrup and transfer the mustard to a clean 8-ounce mason jar with a tight-fitting lid. Seal the jar and let it stand at room temperature about 24 hours before enjoying. The mustard will keep in a tightly sealed container in the refrigerator for up to 3 months.

TIP

You can use half brown and half yellow mustard seed if you wish.

DASHI MAYONNAISE

MAKES ABOUT 1 CUP

Dashi is the master stock of Japan. At its simplest, it includes kombu (dried kelp) and *katsuobushi* (shaved dried bonito) steeped in almost boiling water. This recipe calls for a dashi-infused vinegar to yield a mayonnaise that is guaranteed to make everything taste better. It keeps fresh in the fridge for up to 1 week, but I doubt it will last that long.

1 egg yolk

½ teaspoon kosher salt

1 teaspoon mirin

2 tablespoons Dashi Vinegar (page 38), or store-bought

1 cup vegetable oil

1. In a medium nonreactive bowl, whisk together the egg yolk, salt, and mirin. Stir in half of the dashi vinegar.

2. Whisking constantly, begin adding the oil a few drops at a time. Once the mixture starts to come together, add more oil in a thin stream until you've incorporated half of the oil.

3. Stir in the rest of the vinegar and continue whisking while adding the rest of the oil until fully emulsified. Pour the mixture into a clean pint–sized mason jar with a tight-fitting lid. Seal the jar and let the mayonnaise stand at room temperature for 1 to 2 hours before serving (the vinegar will kill any harmful bacteria in the yolk at room temperature). The mayonnaise will keep in a tightly sealed container in the refrigerator for up to 1 month.

BBQ SAUCE

MAKES ABOUT 2 CUPS

Barbecue, BBQ, or 'cue means something different depending on where you're from, what you style grew up with, and how you like your meat. I don't come from any of the grand Southern traditions, but I do know that I like this sauce. It's delicious on just about anything, and I always keep some on hand in the summer. Throw some chicken on the grill next to a few ears of corn and finish the chicken with this sauce (just at the end; otherwise it will scorch). A perfect summer meal doesn't get easier than this.

2 cups ketchup

1 cup homemade apple cider vinegar (page 27), or store-bought

½ cup molasses

¼ cup packed dark brown sugar

1 tablespoon freshly ground black pepper

½ tablespoon kosher salt

¼ cup finely minced onion

1 tablespoon mustard powder, such as Colman's

1 tablespoon fresh lemon juice

1 tablespoon Worcestershire sauce

1. In a large nonreactive saucepan, combine the ketchup, vinegar, molasses, brown sugar, pepper, salt, onion, mustard powder, lemon juice, and Worcestershire, and bring to a simmer over low heat.

2. Cook the sauce for 90 minutes, stirring occasionally and maintaining a low temperature so the bottom does not scorch.

3. Remove the pan from the heat and let the sauce cool to room temperature. Pack the sauce into a clean mason jar. The sauce will keep in a tightly sealed container in the refrigerator for up to 2 months.

GROUND CHERRY CHUTNEY

MAKES ABOUT 1 PINT

Ground cherries (also called cape gooseberries) are sweet little fruits that grow wrapped in papery husks like their relative the tomatillo. Sweet, tart, and rich—and about the size of large blueberries—these make a great chutney, standing up well to cinnamon and cardamom. Spread this chutney on a grilled cheese made with sharp cheddar on sourdough, and serve the sandwich with your favorite tomato soup for a new take on the comfort-food combo that's perfect for a rainy day.

2 pounds husked and rinsed ground cherries

1½ cups sugar

1 teaspoon kosher salt, plus more to taste

½ cup red wine

1 cup homemade red wine vinegar (page 27), or store-bought

1 cup minced red onion

1 cup black seedless raisins

¼ cup shredded fresh ginger or 1 teaspoon ground

1 tablespoon coriander seed

2 green cardamom pods

1 tablespoon yellow mustard seed

1 whole clove

1 teaspoon crushed red pepper flakes (optional)

½ teaspoon ground cinnamon

1. In a medium nonreactive saucepan, combine the ground cherries, sugar, salt, wine, vinegar, onion, raisins, and ginger; bring to a simmer over medium heat, stirring frequently.

2. Meanwhile, in a small skillet, toast the coriander, cardamom, mustard, clove, and pepper flakes, if using, over low heat until fragrant. Remove the cardamom pods and set them aside.

3. Using a mortar and pestle, grind the spices with the cinnamon and a pinch of salt. Add the spices and the cardamom pods to the simmering ground cherries.

4. Cook the chutney over medium low stirring frequently until it is the consistency of thick jam, 30 to 45 minutes. Discard the cardamom pods and serve, or store in a clean pint-sized mason jar with a tight-fitting lid. Follow the steps on page 66 for water-bath canning to make it shelf stable, processing for 10 minutes. The chutney will keep in a tightly sealed container in the refrigerator for up to 3 months.

SHISO MIGNONETTE

MAKES ABOUT 1 CUP

I learned how to open oysters when I was about eleven. They were a regular treat in our house, and I was more than happy to help prep them, because that meant I could eat as many as I wanted while shucking. I've always eschewed cocktail sauce on oysters—there is absolutely no reason for slathering it on such a nuanced food. For oysters, you need something more refined and less sugary; when a squeeze of lemon juice won't cut it, try this twist on mignonette. This also works well on grilled squid if raw oysters aren't your thing.

⅓ cup Shiso Vinegar (page 34), or store-bought

2 tablespoons mirin

1 shallot, minced

1 tablespoon coarsely ground black pepper

1 teaspoon kosher salt

2 tablespoons minced fresh green shiso leaves

In a small nonreactive bowl, mix together the vinegar, mirin, shallot, pepper, salt, and shiso. Serve immediately or store it in a tightly sealed container in the refrigerator for up to 1 month.

ROASTED HOT SAUCE

MAKES ABOUT 1 QUART

Hot sauce has so many variations that it can make your head spin. This recipe uses roasted tomatoes for a richness of flavor to complement the heat of the peppers. You can sub in whatever chiles you have on hand; a mix of jalapeño, Scotch bonnet, and Fresno is my favorite combo. You can vary the heat based on the amount of seeds you leave in the sauce. This is a good recipe to make on that side burner of your outdoor grill, if you have one, so you don't fill your house with pepper fumes.

12 hot chiles (the more variety, the better)

4 large ripe tomatoes, stems and hard cores removed

2 cups homemade white wine vinegar (page 27) or apple cider vinegar (page 27), or store-bought

½ cup sugar

1 tablespoon grated fresh ginger

1 tablespoon smoked paprika

1 tablespoon kosher salt

1 bay leaf

2 black cardamom pods

½ tablespoon coriander seed

1 teaspoon whole black peppercorns

1. Preheat the oven to 450°F.

2. Place the chiles and tomatoes on a sheet pan and roast until blistered, about 12 minutes. Remove from the oven and let cool.

3. Wearing rubber gloves (see Tips), rub off the skin of the chiles, halve them, and remove as many seeds as you can.

4. In a large nonreactive saucepan, combine the chiles, tomatoes, vinegar, sugar, ginger, paprika, and salt. Make a cheesecloth sachet of the bay leaf, cardamom, coriander, and peppercorns, and add it to the saucepan. Bring the mixture to a simmer over low heat and cook for 30 minutes (see Tips).

5. Remove and discard the sachet and, using an immersion blender, blend the hot sauce until smooth; alternatively, you can slowly pour the sauce into a food processor or blender and process until smooth (be careful when blending hot liquids). Pour the hot sauce into a clean quart-sized mason jar with a tight-fitting lid or smaller narrow mouth glass bottles for serving. You can pack into half-pint

mason jars and follow the steps on page 66 for water-bath canning to make it shelf stable, processing for 10 minutes. The hot sauce will keep tightly sealed in the refrigerator for up to 6 months (or until you move out).

TIPS

I recommend wearing gloves while making this recipe. Also be careful not to stick your face over the pan when the sauce is cooking—a nose full of capsaicin won't do you any favors. You may even want to wear goggles.

QUICK GRILL SAUCE

MAKES ABOUT ½ CUP

This recipe comes together quickly for a sweet sauce you can brush on chicken or pork while finishing the meat on the grill.

2 tablespoons Real Mustard (page 91), or store-bought

4 tablespoons honey

2 tablespoons melted butter

2 tablespoons homemade malt (beer) vinegar (page 27), or store bought

Kosher salt

Freshly ground black pepper

In a small nonreactive bowl, whisk together the mustard, honey, butter, and vinegar, and season to taste with salt and pepper. Use immediately.

STARTERS, MAINS, AND SIDES

While I don't expect you to cook exclusively from this book, I do hope that you'll learn just how much vinegar can change your kitchen repertoire. Acetic acid is a cook's best secret for adding depth of flavor to just about any dish. Try adding ½ cup of vinegar to your chicken or beef stock as it's simmering on the stove; you'll release minerals in the bones and brighten your stock right from the get-go. In many of the following recipes, vinegar takes the front burner and adds to the flavor and the nose of the dish. Hopefully by now you've come to love the sting of vinegar fumes like I do—and when you remove the cover on the pot, you lean in a little to get that punch that tells you that something great will soon be ready. Many of these are dishes that originally were born of necessity at a time when refrigeration was not as dependable (or was nonexistent). We now have the pleasure and the benefit of all these things at our fingertips—and we don't need to rely on vinegar for much more than making a meal more delicious.

DEVILED PICKLED EGGS

SERVES 4 TO 6

I wouldn't have thought that anything could be better than deviled eggs, but starting with pickled eggs really takes this recipe over the top. You'll totally win over colleagues at your company picnic with these bad boys. I use a few of the recipes from the book here, but you could substitute any good-quality mayonnaise and mustard.

8 Pickled Eggs (page 73), halved lengthwise

⅓ cup Dashi Mayonnaise (page 94), or store-bought mayonnaise

1 teaspoon Real Mustard (page 91), or store-bought Dijon mustard

1 teaspoon store-bought distilled white vinegar

¼ teaspoon kosher salt

Freshly ground black pepper

1 tablespoon chives sliced into ¾-inch pieces for garnish

1. Slice the eggs in half lengthwise and carefully remove the yolks from the pickled eggs. Add to a bowl, and place the egg whites on a serving platter.

2. Mash the yolks finely and add the mayonnaise, mustard, vinegar, salt, and pepper to taste. Mix well.

3. Spoon or pipe (using a piping bag or ziplock bag with the corner cut off) the mixture into the whites. Sprinkle with the chives and serve.

DEVILED PICKLED EGGS (PAGE 103)

SALT AND VINEGAR BOILED PEANUTS

SERVES 12

These make a fun party snack, and, much like pistachios and lobsters, somehow the work required to get to the food makes it taste better. You can add a jalapeño or other hot chile to the peanuts while they're cooking to provide some kick. Serve with cold beer—preferably on a Southern porch. This recipe scales well; if you're feeding a whole football team, use a giant stockpot to make a much larger batch.

1 cup kosher salt

1½ cups homemade vinegar of your choice (apple cider, sherry, or other fruit vinegars all work well; see pages 25–39), or store-bought

2 pounds raw peanuts in the shell, soaked in water for 4 to 8 hours and drained (see Tip)

2 tablespoons honey

1 to 2 jalapeños or other hot chile (such as Thai chile), fresh or dried (optional)

TIP

While you don't have to presoak the peanuts, they will cook faster this way.

1. Fill an 8-quart nonreactive stockpot two-thirds full with water and add the salt. Bring to a simmer over medium-high heat and stir to dissolve the salt.

2. Add the vinegar, peanuts, honey, and jalapeño, if using. Bring to a boil over medium-high heat and then lower to a simmer and loosely cover the pot. Continue to simmer the peanuts, stirring them every once in a while.

3. Taste the peanuts after 2 hours to check the texture; they should still be a little springy but not mushy. Keep simmering them until they reach your desired texture, this may take up to 4 hours total. When the peanuts are done, remove the stockpot from the heat and let the peanuts stand in the water for 1 hour.

4. Drain the peanuts and serve while still warm with icy beer, or enjoy them cold. The peanuts will keep in a tightly sealed container in the refrigerator for up to 2 weeks.

SEAWEED SALAD

SERVES 4

This ubiquitous sushi side dish is easy to make at home, and it even skips the MSG that's often found in the restaurant version. Seaweed is a sustainable superfood and has tons of flavor.

1 ounce mixed dried seaweed (see Tip)

2 tablespoons homemade rice (sake) vinegar (page 27) or Dashi Vinegar (page 38), or store-bought

1 teaspoon soy sauce

1 teaspoon toasted sesame oil

1 teaspoon sugar

½ teaspoon kosher salt

1 teaspoon grated fresh ginger

1 tablespoon toasted sesame seeds

1 whole scallion, chopped thin on the bias (white and green parts)

1. Place the dried seaweed in a small bowl and add plenty of water to cover; let it soak for about 10 minutes to rehydrate the seaweed.

2. Meanwhile, in a medium nonreactive bowl, whisk together the vinegar, soy sauce, sesame oil, sugar, salt, and ginger.

3. Drain the seaweed and add it to the bowl with the dressing. Toss to combine the ingredients.

4. Garnish the salad with the sesame seeds and sliced scallion, and serve immediately.

TIP

You can find mixed dried seaweed in most health food stores and Asian groceries.

KALE SALAD

SERVES 4

This is a go-to recipe that can be adapted for any time of year: it's hearty enough for winter, but because it requires no heat, it also works well in summer. Bring your kids in the kitchen to help with the prep; as long as the kale leaves are torn, size doesn't really matter. Top this salad with steak for a heartier meal that doubles down on iron.

2 teaspoons kosher salt

1 bunch of Tuscan kale, thick stems removed and leaves torn into bite-sized pieces

¼ cup store-bought sherry vinegar

3 ounces feta or chèvre

3 or 4 peaches, plums, or other stone fruit, pitted and sliced

¼ cup extra-virgin olive oil

Pinch of crushed red pepper flakes

1. In a large nonreactive bowl, massage the salt into the kale. Let the kale macerate with the salt for 5 to 10 minutes.

2. Add the vinegar and massage the kale a few times more, then toss in the cheese, fruit, olive oil, and pepper flakes. Serve immediately.

CLABBERED-MILK BLINI
WITH CURED FISH

SERVES 6 AS AN APPETIZER

Clabbered milk refers to unpasteurized whole milk that, when left at room temperature under a specific humidity, thickens and sours because of the bacteria in the raw milk. Historically, this was a great preservation option for milk, and it would keep in this state far longer than fresh milk that had been cooled in the fridge. As such, the fermentation tang became a common flavor that appeared in cakes and other baked goods. You can use vinegar to quickly clabber milk and add that slightly sour taste as well as a thickened texture. I like these blini as a savory base for cured fish (opposite page) or caviar. Or you can sweeten things up with a Nutella topping or Vinegar Compote (page 144).

1 tablespoon homemade apple cider vinegar (page 27), or store-bought

1¼ cups whole milk

1 large egg

1 cup all-purpose flour

1 teaspoon sugar

Pinch of kosher salt

Unsalted butter, for the griddle

Cured Fish (opposite page), smoked salmon or trout, or caviar, for serving

Crème fraîche, for serving

1. Pour the vinegar and milk into a non-reactive bowl or 2-cup measure; stir to combine. Let rest for about 10 minutes, or until the milk starts to thicken.

2. Whisk the egg into the clabbered milk; add the flour, sugar, and salt to combine. Let the batter rest for 10 minutes.

3. Heat a griddle over medium heat and grease with butter. Drop the batter by the spoonful onto the griddle to make 2-inch cakes. Cook until lightly browned 1-2 minutes on each side, removing each cake to a plate when done. Keep warm, with a tea towel, or in a low oven while you finish cooking the rest of the batter, greasing the griddle between batches.

4. Top the blini with cured fish and crème fraîche, and serve.

CURED FISH

SERVES 8 AS AN APPETIZER

Mackerel are a prolific fish on the New England coast, and I have spent countless hours catching them on summer vacations and figuring out what to do with them. I love curing the fillets and serving them as sushi, though it took me years to finally get this recipe right. It's very simple, but the sugar wasn't an obvious ingredient in the fish I'd eaten in Japanese restaurants. I learned that rather than just adding sweetness, the sugar seasons the fish and draws out moisture the same way salt does. Top sushi rice (page 133) with this for nigiri sushi, or slice it up and serve on bagels or as part of a pickle platter for brunch.

3 whole mackerel, filleted, or 6 fillets about 2 pounds total (see Tip)

1 cup sugar

1 cup kosher salt

1 cup homemade rice (sake) vinegar (page 27), or store-bought

TIP

If filleting whole fish, don't pull out the pin bones yet. It will be much easier to do after you cure the fish; if the fillets are small and the bones thin, they'll soften in the cure and can be left in and eaten.

1. In a glass or enamel shallow roasting pan, cover the fillets with the sugar and let stand for at least 1 hour but not more than 2 hours.

2. Rinse off the sugar, pat the fish dry, and return them to the pan. Cover the fish with the salt. Again, let the fish stand for at least 1 hour and up to 2 hours.

3. Rinse the fish again, and add them to a ziplock bag that fits the fillets snugly and cover with the vinegar. Push out as much air as possible, seal the bag, and refrigerate at least overnight but not more than 24 hours.

4. Remove the fish from the bag, and rinse and pat them dry. Pull out any large pin bones you can still feel and discard. Slice and serve. The fish will keep in a tightly sealed container in the refrigerator for up to 1 week.

MINT PESTO
WITH RADIATORI

SERVES 4 TO 6

There's almost nothing that tastes more like early fall to me than pasta with pesto on a warm night. I love the way radiatori hold sauce, but you can use any short pasta for this dish. Serve with a perky super-cold rosé. You can swap toasted walnuts for the pepitas if you want an earthier dish. This pesto recipe freezes well, especially in ice-cube trays that make for easy portioning. You can substitute basil here, but I find the mint super refreshing.

Kosher salt

¼ cup toasted pepitas

2 garlic cloves

3 cups lightly packed mint leaves, washed and well dried

½ cup good-quality olive oil

¼ cup homemade white wine vinegar (page 27) or Fruit Vinegar (page 33), or store-bought

Freshly ground black pepper

1 pound dried radiatori pasta

Freshly grated Parmesan cheese, for serving

1. Bring a large pot of water to a boil over high heat and add a few tablespoons of salt.

2. Place the pepitas and garlic in a food processor or blender and pulse until finely chopped.

3. Add the mint, oil, and vinegar, and process until finely chopped, scraping down the sides as needed. Add salt and pepper to taste. Remove the pesto to a large nonreactive serving bowl.

4. Add the pasta to the pot of boiling water and cook to your desired level of doneness according to the package instructions. Drain the pasta and toss with the pesto while hot. Serve with freshly grated Parmesan.

MY ONION SOUP

SERVES 8 TO 10

This is comfort food of the highest order—with cheesy bread, rich broth, and a side of Julia Child for good measure. In episode 97 of TV's *The French Chef*, Julia Child makes onion soup for a spectacular show with an opener about the value of a good chef's knife and how to care for it. This recipe is informed by her methods but adds vinegar for a brightness that is sometimes lacking in onion soup. Your house will smell amazing as the onions turn from translucent to caramel—and you'll be happy to know that this is easy to make for a crowd.

4 tablespoons (½ stick) unsalted butter, plus more for the baguette

2 tablespoons extra-virgin olive oil

8 cups thinly sliced yellow onions (about 4 large onions)

2 teaspoons kosher salt, plus more to taste

2 teaspoons sugar

6 tablespoons all-purpose flour

2 quarts hot Homemade Stock (page 116)

1½ cups dry white wine

2 bay leaves

½ teaspoon minced fresh sage

Freshly ground black pepper

1 baguette

A medium piece of Comté or Gruyère cheese

8 to 10 teaspoons homemade red wine vinegar (page 27) or Honey Vinegar (page 31), or store-bought, for serving

1. Melt the butter and the olive oil together over medium-low heat in a large enameled Dutch oven or heavy-bottomed stainless-steel stockpot. Add the onions, cover the pot, and cook, stirring occasionally, for about 20 minutes, or until the onions are translucent.

2. Remove the cover and add the salt and the sugar. Raise the heat to medium-high and cook, stirring frequently, for about 30 minutes, or until the onions are a golden brown.

3. Lower the heat to medium and add the flour; stir to combine. Cook for 2 minutes to brown the flour lightly.

4. Add about 1 cup of the stock and whisk to combine with the flour and onions. Add the rest of the stock, the wine, bay leaves, and sage. Bring to a simmer over medium heat.

5. Continue to simmer slowly for 30 minutes and season to taste with salt and pepper. Remove the bay leaves.

6. Preheat the oven to 325°F. While the soup simmers, cut the baguette into 1-inch slices, one for each serving bowl, spread one side of each with butter, place on a baking sheet, and toast in the oven. Once the toasts are browned, about 4 minutes, place a slice of cheese on each piece and bake until the cheese is melted, about 2 minutes more.

7. To serve, in each bowl place one cheesy baguette slice, ladle with soup to cover, and pour 1 teaspoon of vinegar over the top.

TIP

When you're tasting a sauce, soup, or other dish at home and it's missing something, your first instinct might be to reach for the salt. Try adding vinegar instead. Often what's missing isn't sodium, but a little more acid. You can thank me later.

HOMEMADE STOCK

MAKES 4 QUARTS

Adding vinegar to the water when making stock will help pull more nutrients and minerals out of the bones. The acid softens the bones and, of course, adds brightness to your finished product. I find that red wine vinegar or sherry vinegar is the best match for meat broths. As for the bones, I like to use a mix of beef, chicken, pork, and lamb (the ratio is up to you, but that's my preferred order and you can of course do a single bone stock), and let them simmer for at least a few hours. Make sure to taste and adjust the salt before using or drinking this.

4 pounds bones with some meat still attached

2 bay leaves

½ tablespoon whole black peppercorns

½ cup homemade red wine vinegar (page 27), or store-bought sherry vinegar

2 celery stalks, roughly chopped

2 carrots, roughly chopped

1 unpeeled red onion, roughly chopped

1. Place the bones in a large nonreactive stockpot and cover them with cold water by at least 1 inch. Add the bay leaves and peppercorns. Bring to a boil over high heat and boil for 5 minutes, skimming and discarding any foam that appears on the surface.

2. Add the vinegar, celery, carrots, and onion. Bring back to a boil, then reduce the heat to simmer uncovered for 3 to 5 hours.

3. Strain and cool the stock; store, covered, in the fridge overnight. Skim any fat that has solidified on the surface. Use within 4 days or freeze (see Tip) for up to 6 months.

TIP

Divide the stock among pint- or quart-sized deli containers before freezing so you always have the quantity you need on hand.

FISH AND LATKES

SERVES 6

Vinegar makes a great condiment on its own; fish-and-chips need little else than a good-quality malt (beer) vinegar (see page 27). In Japan, vinegar is the preferred accompaniment for shellfish and crustaceans. At a recent lobster dinner, a friend from Tokyo remarked that butter was such an odd dip for lobster. By the end of the meal, we were all converts to vinegar. Without the butter to coat our mouths, we could really taste the succulent brininess of the meat.

FISH BATTER

⅔ cup all-purpose flour

2 tablespoons paprika (smoked, if you'd like)

1 teaspoon kosher salt

1 teaspoon freshly ground black pepper

1 large egg

½ cup cold lager beer

¼ cup ice water

¼ cup homemade malt (beer) vinegar (page 27), or store-bought

LATKES

3 pounds russet potatoes, scrubbed well

1 medium onion

2 teaspoons kosher salt

2 large eggs

2 tablespoons all-purpose flour

1 teaspoon freshly ground black pepper

Vegetable oil or lard, for frying

1. Make the Batter: In a medium nonreactive bowl, mix the flour, paprika, salt, and pepper. In another medium nonreactive bowl, beat the egg and pour in the beer, ice water, and vinegar, and mix well. Pour the liquid into the dry ingredients and mix well. (You can make the batter a few days ahead of time and store it in the fridge in a covered container until you're ready to begin frying.)

2. Prepare the Latkes: Grate the potatoes and onion into a colander placed over a large bowl to catch the liquid that drains. Sprinkle in the salt and gently massage everything together. Let the mixture stand over the bowl for 10 minutes to drain.

3. In a separate large bowl, beat the eggs and add the flour and pepper. Squeeze out as much juice as you can from the potatoes and onion, and then add them to the egg mixture. Pour off the liquid from the bowl that the potatoes drained into and discard it, reserving the white starch that settles at the bottom of the bowl and scraping it into the potato mixture; mix well.

RECIPE CONTINUES

FISH

2 pounds pollack, cod, dogfish, or other firm fish fillets, cut into 2-inch-square pieces (see Tip)

Homemade malt (beer) vinegar (page 27) or store-bought, for serving

Kosher salt, for serving

TIP

Frying at home can be a pain. But if you follow a few simple tips, your food can be delicious and not soggy:

- Make sure to keep your oil at a hot enough temperature, in this case 365°F.

- The colder the ingredients start out, the better (though they should not be frozen).

- I prefer dogfish, pollack, or lingcod.

- Use sturdy russet potatoes and scrub them well.

4. Preheat the oven to 225°F.

5. Pour the oil at least 1-inch deep into a cast-iron skillet, Dutch oven, or electric skillet. Heat the oil to 365°F. Add ¼ cup of the potatoes at a time to the hot oil to make 2- to 3-inch latkes and fry until golden brown, turning once, 3 to 4 minutes per side. Remove the latkes to drain on paper towels or a rack and keep them warm in the oven. Repeat with the remaining potatoes, bringing the oil back up to temperature between batches.

6. Fry the Fish: Add more oil to the skillet so it is at least 1-inch deep and heat it to 365°F. Dredge the fish squares in the prepared batter and then add them to the oil, turning once until golden brown, 3 to 4 minutes per side. Leave 1 to 2 inches between the pieces as you fry; it's better to fry in batches than to crowd the pan. Drain the fish on paper towels and repeat with the rest of the fish, bringing the oil back up to temperature between batches.

7. Serve the fish with the latkes, generous amounts of malt vinegar, and a sprinkle of salt.

GERMAN-STYLE MASHED POTATOES
(PAGE 130)

SAUCY PIQUANT PORK CHOPS

SERVES 4

Adapted from Edward Giobbi's *Italian Family Cooking*, published in 1971, these chops were a staple in my mother's cooking. Ed Giobbi lived across the street from us in Katonah, New York, when I was growing up, and he kept chickens, peacocks, and hens. Every time my mother made this dish, she told the story about how our dog Max would venture across the street and terrorize Ed's birds. When I moved out on my own, I found this in the family recipe book my mother gave me, and it's been part of my own repertoire ever since. I like to serve these with roasted or mashed potatoes and a nice salad.

1 tablespoon unsalted butter

4 bone-in pork chops
(each 1 to 2 inches thick)

½ cup finely diced onion

1 tablespoon all-purpose flour

1 cup Homemade Stock
(page 116), or store-bought

¼ cup homemade red wine
vinegar (page 27), or
store-bought

¼ cup store-bought balsamic
vinegar (not the expensive,
thick "extra vecchio")

2 tablespoons capers, rinsed
if salted

2 tablespoons cornichons,
cut into caper-sized pieces

¼ cup chopped flat-leaf parsley

Kosher salt

Freshly ground black pepper

1. Preheat the oven to 400°F.

2. In a large cast-iron skillet with a lid, melt the butter over medium heat. When the foam subsides, brown the chops on all sides, about 2 minutes per side, being careful not to scorch the butter.

3. Remove the chops to a plate and pour off all but a tablespoon of the fat. Add the onion and cook over medium heat, stirring often, until they start to brown, about 8 minutes.

4. Add the flour and stir. Cook for 1 minute, then add the stock, vinegars, capers, cornichons, and half of the parsley. Simmer the sauce for 3 minutes.

5. Pour the sauce into a bowl. Return the chops to the pan, cover, and bake for 15 minutes.

6. Remove the chops from the pan and set aside to rest for 5 minutes. Add the sauce to the pan and, over medium heat, reduce it by a fourth to thicken, about 2 minutes. Slice the chops and spoon the sauce over the meat. Season with salt and pepper to taste, and serve.

SAUERBRATEN

SERVES 8

Originally born out of a need to preserve the meat from the hunt, this cooking method is used today to soften and flavor what are traditionally cheaper and tougher cuts of the animal. By marinating a cheap bottom round in vinegar and spices and then cooking it in those juices, you get a mouthwatering German-style pot roast. Though I never went to the legendary German restaurant Lüchow's on East 14th Street in Manhattan, which closed in 1982, this recipe uses their secret: adding crushed ginger cookies to thicken the gravy after the roast is done. This can be cooked just as easily on the second or fourth day of brining if your schedule demands it; just know that the longer you let the meat sit, the tangier it will get. This recipe goes great with German-Style Mashed Potatoes (page 130) and Roasted Red Cabbage (page 128).

1 cup homemade red wine vinegar (page 27), or store-bought

1 cup amber ale (see Tip)

1 medium onion, sliced

1 large carrot, chopped

1 celery stalk, chopped

4 whole cloves

10 juniper berries, smashed with the side of a knife

2 bay leaves

1 tablespoon kosher salt

1 teaspoon whole black peppercorns

1 bottom round roast (3 to 4 pounds)

3 tablespoons extra-virgin olive oil

1 cup finely crushed old-fashioned gingersnap cookies

⅓ cup sour cream

½ cup seedless raisins (optional)

1. In an enameled Dutch oven or stainless-steel pot large enough to hold the bottom round, combine 2 cups of water, the vinegar, ale, onion, carrot, celery, cloves, juniper berries, bay leaves, salt, and peppercorns, stirring to dissolve the salt. Place the meat into the pot and store in the refrigerator for 3 days, turning daily if the liquid doesn't completely cover the roast.

2. On the third day, remove the pot from the fridge and preheat the oven to 325°F.

3. Remove the bottom round from the liquid and pat it dry. In a cast-iron or other heavy skillet over medium-high heat, heat the olive oil and brown the roast on all sides, about 3 minutes per side.

4. Bring the liquid in the Dutch oven to a simmer over medium heat and carefully return the browned roast to the pot. Cover and move to the oven; cook until tender, about 3 hours.

5. Remove the pot from the oven and place the roast on a cutting board to let it rest. Meanwhile, strain the solids from the cooking liquid and return the liquid to the pot, reserving the carrot, celery, and any onion pieces that aren't completely mushy, and discarding any cloves, the bay leaves, and other spices.

6. Boil the sauce over high heat to reduce by a third, about 10 minutes. Reduce the heat to low and stir in the crushed gingersnaps, a little at a time, whisking until all the pieces are dissolved and you reach a gravy-like consistency (depending on the amount of liquid, you may not need all of the cookies). Add the sour cream and the raisins, if using.

7. Slice the roast, plate with the vegetables, and pour the sauce over the meat to serve.

TIP

Choose a beer that's not too hoppy (no IPAs); the bitterness will only make the meat taste astringent. Instead, stick with the theme of this meal and opt for a German beer. If you don't have beer, wine will do just fine.

ROAST CHICKEN ADOBO

SERVES 4 TO 6

In the Philippines, where this recipe originates, they use palm vinegar, which is made from the sap of palm coconut trees. Use it if you have it; otherwise, apple cider or pineapple vinegar is a good substitute. The vinegar cuts down on unwanted bacteria while marinating the meat. Usually served as a stew using dark meat, this recipe has been adapted for a classic whole roast chicken. Serve over rice with the hot pan sauce on the side.

1 cup store-bought palm vinegar or homemade apple cider vinegar (page 27 or pineapple vinegar (page 33), or store-bought

½ cup soy sauce

1 teaspoon fish sauce

1 head of garlic, peeled and minced

2 bay leaves or 2 teaspoons herbes de Provence

Freshly ground black pepper

1 whole chicken (3 to 4 pounds)

2 tablespoons all-purpose flour

Cooked rice, for serving

TIP

If you plan on cooking the dish within 3 hours, you can marinate the chicken at room temperature. Also, these ingredients easily double to make two chickens for serving a crowd.

1. In a small nonreactive bowl, mix together the vinegar, soy sauce, fish sauce, garlic, bay leaves, and pepper. Place the chicken in a large zip-top bag. Pour the vinegar mixture over the chicken and seal, pressing out as much air as possible.

2. Marinate the chicken for at least 2 hours or up to overnight in the refrigerator (the longer the better), turning the bag a few times (see Tip).

3. Preheat the oven to 400°F.

4. Take the chicken out of the bag, discard the bay leaves, and reserve the marinade. Let the chicken come to room temperature in a roasting pan, about 30 minutes. Roast the chicken for 15 minutes, then reduce the heat to 350°F. Cook for about 30 more minutes until the breast meat registers 165°F on an instant-read thermometer.

5. Remove the chicken to a cutting board to rest for 10 minutes. Add the reserved marinade to the roasting pan with the juices and boil the liquid to reduce it by half, about 8 minutes. Sprinkle in the flour and whisk to combine.

6. Serve the chicken with the rice and sauce.

STEWED LAMB NECK

SERVES 8

This is a hearty meal for a chilly afternoon. Use a pressure cooker to cut the cooking time to less than an hour and you can make this dish on a weeknight. If time is of little object, you can simmer it on the stove for 3 to 4 hours and achieve similar results; however, I find that the pressure cooker also aids in pulling more gelatin from the bones and connective tissue, yielding a far more unctuous dish.

Kosher salt

Freshly ground black pepper

3 pounds lamb neck with bones (ask your butcher to cut for stew; see Tip)

2 tablespoons extra-virgin olive oil

2 medium onions, chopped

1 thumb-sized piece of ginger, peeled and minced

4 garlic cloves, smashed and peeled

2 carrots, chopped

1 celery stalk, chopped

2 thyme sprigs

1 bay leaf

1 rosemary sprig

½ teaspoon cumin seeds, toasted

1 quart Homemade Stock (page 116) or water

¼ cup homemade red wine vinegar (page 27), or store-bought sherry vinegar

1 pound wide egg noodles

2 tablespoons (¼ stick) unsalted butter

1. Season the lamb neck with salt and pepper. In a 6- to 8-quart pressure cooker (or Dutch oven if taking the slow route), heat the olive oil over medium-high heat until shimmering. Brown the lamb in batches, about 3 minutes, and set aside.

2. Add the onions and ginger to the pressure cooker (or Dutch oven) and cook over medium heat until the onion is translucent, about 5 minutes. Add the garlic and cook for about 1 minute, or until fragrant. Add the carrots, celery, and herbs and seeds, and cook for about 5 minutes, stirring frequently, or until they just start to soften and the carrots are bright orange.

3. Return the lamb to the pressure cooker (or Dutch oven) and add the stock and vinegar. Bring to a simmer over medium heat and cover (don't let it boil). Cook the lamb on high according to the pressure cooker directions (approximately 15 pounds of pressure) for 30 minutes. Remove from the heat and let the pressure come down naturally (or use the quick method appropriate for your pressure cooker).

4. When the pressure has depleted, open the cooker and remove the lamb to a large nonreactive bowl to rest for 10 minutes. Season the stew with salt and pepper to taste. If it's too watery for your preference, you can boil the liquid to reduce it.

5. While the meat rests bring a medium stockpot of water to a boil over high heat, salt it, and add the noodles, cooking them according to the package directions.

6. Meanwhile, remove the meat from the bones and return it to the pot, stirring to coat.

7. When the noodles are just tender, drain them well and immediately place them in a medium bowl with the butter. Toss to combine.

8. Serve the stewed lamb over the egg noodles and enjoy.

TIP

If you can find it, goat meat, which often comes already cut into small chunks, is a great substitute for lamb.

ROASTED RED CABBAGE

SERVES 10

This recipe is so simple and makes a delicious snack with beer. Or turn it into a great side by serving it with Sauerbraten (page 122) or Japanese noodles. I'd eat it with just about anything. The crispier the cabbage gets in the oven, the better the flavor!

1 medium head of red cabbage (about 3 pounds), cored and leaves separated, cut into bite-sized pieces

⅓ cup extra-virgin olive oil

Homemade apple cider vinegar (page 27), or store-bought

Kosher salt

1. Preheat the oven to 425°F.

2. Place the cabbage pieces in a non-reactive bowl with the oil and toss to combine. Spread the cabbage on a sheet pan and roast until the thinner leaves are brown and crispy, about 30 minutes.

3. Remove the pan from the oven and spray the vinegar on the hot cabbage. Sprinkle with salt to taste and serve.

TIP

Putting a spray top on your vinegar bottle will allow you to evenly cover the cabbage with vinegar.

GERMAN-STYLE MASHED POTATOES

SERVES 8

My first "real" job in high school was at a deli in Petaluma, California, which was famous for its potato salad. The secret lay in the dry spice mix that we added to the homemade mayonnaise. Though the exact recipe for the mix was a closely guarded secret, this recipe is nowhere near as fussy, makes better use of vinegar, and features the potatoes mashed until creamy. Serve this dish alongside good grainy mustard, sauerkraut, and hearty sausages for an easy German-style feast. I like to leave the skin on the potatoes for the added texture, but feel free to peel them, especially if the potatoes aren't as new as you'd like.

3 pounds new potatoes, peeled if desired

4 tablespoons kosher salt, plus more to taste

⅓ cup homemade apple cider vinegar (page 27) or Chive Blossom Vinegar (page 39), or store-bought

⅓ cup extra-virgin olive oil

2 tablespoons (¼ stick) unsalted butter

Freshly ground black pepper

2 scallions, thinly sliced on the bias (green parts only), for garnish

TIP

This recipe is a spin-off of traditional German potato salad, which can easily be made instead by reducing the cooking time of the potatoes a few minutes (cook them until soft, but still firm). Cube or slice them, then dress with the ingredients before serving cold or warm.

1. Quarter the potatoes, place them in a stockpot, and cover with water by 1 inch. Add the salt. Bring the potatoes to a boil, turn down the heat to medium high, and cook them for about 10 minutes, or until a fork can easily pierce them.

2. Drain the potatoes and place them in a large nonreactive bowl. Pour the vinegar over the potatoes while they are still hot and mix well, mashing them with a potato masher or wooden spoon until soft and fluffy.

3. Fold in the olive oil and butter while the potatoes are still warm. Liberally add more salt and pepper to taste.

4. Garnish with the scallions and serve warm.

GREENS WITH PICKLED GARLIC

SERVES 6

Here's a great use for Pickled Whole Garlic (page 81); if you don't have it, you can substitute fresh garlic. Sautéed greens are a natural fit for vinegar. Collards, kale, beet greens—this recipe works for anything you can get your hands on. A trip to Bub's BBQ in Sunderland, Massachusetts, was a favorite outing when I was in college. The portions were huge and the pricing was fair, and on top of that, they had an unlimited sides bar. The collard greens are what I remember most: tender, smoky, and vinegary.

¼ pound bacon or bacon end, chopped

1 red onion, chopped

2 cups chicken broth, lager, or water

⅓ cup homemade malt (beer) vinegar (page 27) or apple cider vinegar (page 27), or store-bought

2 tablespoons good-quality maple syrup or dark brown sugar

1 tablespoon molasses, plus more as desired

1 tart, crunchy apple, cored and chopped

½ teaspoon crushed red pepper flakes

2 pounds collard (or other) greens, stems removed, coarsely chopped

1 head Pickled Whole Garlic (page 81) or 8 fresh garlic cloves, peeled and minced

Kosher salt

Freshly ground black pepper

1. In a heavy skillet with a lid, cook the bacon over medium heat until most of the fat has rendered, but don't let the bacon get too crispy brown. Remove the bacon to a paper towel-lined plate and pour off and discard half of the fat.

2. Sauté the onion over medium-high heat in the bacon fat until slightly browned, about 5 minutes, then add the broth, vinegar, maple syrup, molasses, apple, and pepper flakes. Bring to a simmer over medium heat, and stir in the greens and bacon.

3. Cover and simmer over low heat for 20 minutes.

4. Add the garlic and simmer for 5 more minutes. Season with salt and pepper to taste and adjust the sweetness with more maple syrup or molasses as desired.

SEAWEED SALAD
(PAGE 107)

CURED MACKEREL
(PAGE 111)

QUICK PICKLED CARROT
AND GINGER
(PAGE 76)

SUMESHI (SUSHI RICE) BOWL

Rice is serious business, especially in Japan, where an apprentice chef can take years to perfect his *sushi*. This recipe should get you well on your way to enjoying great rice at home. The goal is to achieve cooked rice grains that are still whole (not crushed), sticky, and slightly glossy. Try your hand at making nigiri sushi, with fish on top of a small piece of rice, but know that you probably need another two years to nail down the proper technique. You can use this rice for maki (rolls) or you can of course stick to more rustic uses like *chirashi* bowls and hand rolls.

2 cups short grain Japanese rice

½ cup homemade rice (sake) vinegar (page 27), or store-bought

2½ tablespoons sugar

2 x 3-inch piece of kombu

Your favorite vegetables, pickled (see pages 65–84), cured mackerel, soft-cooked egg, and/or sliced cooked steak or other fish, for serving

1. Rinse the rice well until you see little to no cloudiness in the water. Add the rice and 2 cups of water to a rice cooker or a medium stovetop saucepan. Follow the directions for the rice cooker, or if cooking the rice on the stovetop, bring the rice to a boil, then immediately reduce to a simmer and cover. Cook for 12 to 15 minutes, until tender. Remove from the heat and let stand covered for 10 minutes.

2. While the rice cooks, bring the vinegar, sugar, and kombu just to a boil in a small nonreactive saucepan and remove from the heat to rest. When the rice is done, transfer it to a large nonreactive bowl or wide dish with 2-inch-high sides (like a lasagna pan). Fluff the rice.

3. Remove the kombu from the vinegar and discard. Sprinkle the vinegar mixture over the rice to evenly coat it. Use a *shamoji* (Japanese rice paddle) for best results or a flat wooden spatula to fold the vinegar into the rice, being careful not to mash the rice. Serve warm with pickled vegetables, fish, soft-cooked egg, and anything else your heart desires.

SQUASH STEAMED OVER VINEGAR

SERVES 6

I go on a steamed squash kick every winter. This recipe is the easiest and fastest way to make this delicious vegetable, which often seems like a big production. Choose a kabocha or acorn squash with soft enough skin and you don't even have to peel it (you can eat the skin, too). Serve this with large flakes of sea salt, soy sauce, wasabi, and sushi rice (see page 133).

1 kabocha or acorn squash (about 2 pounds)

1 cup homemade rice (sake) vinegar (page 27) or red wine vinegar (page 27), or store-bought

1 teaspoon flaky sea salt (I like Maldon)

1. Cut the squash in half and scoop out and discard the seeds. Slice the squash into ½ to ¾-inch-thick crescents.

2. Heat the vinegar over medium high heat in a medium nonreactive saucepan fitted with a steamer insert. When the vinegar boils, add the squash, cover the pot, and steam until tender, 8 to 10 minutes. Sprinkle with sea salt before serving. The squash will keep in a tightly sealed container in the refrigerator for up to 5 days.

DESSERTS

We rarely think of vinegar in desserts, but why not? Tartness is welcome in treats like Key lime pie and lemon sorbet. With vinegar, we have one more ingredient that adds brightness besides citrus. Some recipes, like Vinegar Pie (opposite page), were invented out of necessity by pioneering families looking to flavor their food in the dreary depths of winter when store inventory was low and the possibility of fresh ingredients was still months away. Fruits like strawberries and bananas not only make great vinegars but also play really well with acetic flavors in dessert form. Think thick, goopy balsamic on sweet fresh strawberries—you don't even need a recipe for that. Pour some berry vinegar (page 33) and rum on ripe bananas and ignite the whole thing, or spray some apple cider vinegar on your crème brûlée. There are many ways to keep consuming all things vinegar even at the end of the meal.

VINEGAR PIE

MAKES 1 (9-INCH) PIE

When dried and stored fruit had worn out in winter and early settlers needed something to flavor their pies, they turned to vinegar. I first encountered this dessert in the second book of Laura Ingalls Wilder's famous Little House series, *Farmer Boy*, which takes place during the 1870s in upstate New York, where apple cider vinegar would have been plentiful.

4 large eggs

1 cup sugar

¼ teaspoon ground cinnamon

⅛ teaspoon freshly grated nutmeg

1 tablespoon all-purpose flour

1 tablespoon good-quality maple syrup

⅓ cup homemade apple cider vinegar (page 27), or store-bought

1 Flaky Piecrust, unbaked (page 139)

Whipped cream, for serving

TIP

This is a shallow one-shell pie, so double the recipe to make two, or save your second crust for another open custard-type pie. For a deep pie, multiply the recipe ingredients by one and a half.

1. Preheat the oven to 350°F.

2. In a nonreactive medium bowl, whisk the eggs with ¼ cup of the sugar, the cinnamon, and nutmeg until well blended. Set aside.

3. In a medium nonreactive saucepan whisk together the flour, the remaining ¾ cup sugar, 1 cup of water, the maple syrup, and vinegar. Bring to a boil over medium-high heat, stirring to dissolve the sugar.

4. When the sugar is dissolved, remove the saucepan from the heat and pour the liquid into the egg mixture. Mix well, then return the filling to the saucepan. Cook over low heat, stirring until the custard reaches 175°F; do not boil the custard.

5. On a lightly floured surface, roll out the pie crust to a 13-inch round. Fit it into a 9-inch pie plate. Pour the mixture into the pie shell and bake for 30 to 40 minutes, or until the custard is set and the crust starts to brown.

6. Remove the pie shell from the oven. Cool the pie completely before serving with whipped cream. Pie will keep covered in the refrigerator for up to 3 days.

FLAKY PIECRUST

MAKES 2 (9-INCH) CRUSTS

I learned to make piecrust from Lucinda Ray, a family friend, in the kitchen of her farmhouse on the island of Vinalhaven, Maine. Blueberry was the order of the day, but you can use this crust for anything. The keys to flaky piecrust are not to overwork it and to keep it cold. You can use other vinegars to pair with different fillings.

3 cups all-purpose flour

1 teaspoon kosher salt (see Tips)

1 teaspoon sugar (see Tips)

1 cup (2 sticks) cold unsalted butter, cut into ½-inch cubes

6 tablespoons cold lard or vegetable shortening, cut into ½-inch cubes

2 tablespoons vinegar (white distilled or any kind of homemade)

3 tablespoons ice water

1. In a large nonreactive bowl, mix together the flour, salt, and sugar.

2. Add the butter and lard and cut into the flour with a pastry blender, until the fat is pea-sized and evenly distributed.

3. In a small nonreactive bowl, mix the vinegar and water. Sprinkle the liquid into the flour and shortening, and mix to combine just until the dough comes together.

4. Divide the dough in halves, shape each into a ball, and press them into 2 flat rounds. If using immediately roll them out to ⅛-inch thick. Flat rounds of piecrust will keep wrapped in plastic in the freezer for up to 4 months.

TIPS

You can double the sugar if you're making a sweet pie.

Double the salt if you're using this for a savory pie.

BALSAMIC ICE CREAM

SERVES 4

This dessert is a still-frozen ice cream, or *semifreddo,* as opposed to churned ice cream. While hand-churned ice cream will yield a smoother texture, this recipe works well and requires no special equipment. Serve it with fresh strawberries, raspberries, or blueberries.

---

2 large eggs, separated

½ cup confectioners' sugar

1¼ cups whipping cream

2 tablespoons store-bought balsamic vinegar

½ teaspoon flaky sea salt, such as Maldon

1. Beat the egg yolks, confectioners' sugar, and ¼ cup of the whipping cream in a double boiler. Set the mixture over medium heat and cook until it starts to thicken, about 10 minutes. Chill the custard to room temperature or refrigerate until cool.

2. In a small bowl, whip the remaining 1 cup whipping cream until thick. You can do this by hand with a whisk, an egg beater, or an electric mixer. Stir in the balsamic vinegar and salt. Fold the cooled custard into the whipped cream vinegar mixture.

3. In another bowl—copper if you have it—whisk the egg whites until stiff but not dry. Copper helps the egg whites whip well without becoming dry and grainy.

4. Fold the whipped cream and custard mixture into the egg whites. Pour the mixture into an 8 × 4-inch loaf pan or freeze-safe bowl, cover it, and freeze overnight before serving. This ice cream will last in the freezer well covered for up to 2 weeks.

STRAWBERRY
RHUBARB SHRUB
(PAGE 44)

BLUEBERRY SHRUB
(PAGE 42)

VINEGAR CANDY

MAKES 60 CANDIES

We usually think of vinegar as a savory flavoring, but we should really consider it tart. In many candies, citric acid is used to brighten the sugar. Here we've replaced that with acetic acid, and you can make endless variations based on the type of vinegar used. Vary the vinegar for sherry or red wine candy.

2 tablespoons (¼ stick) unsalted butter, plus more for the pan

2 cups sugar

½ cup homemade apple cider vinegar (page 27) or maple vinegar, or store-bought

½ teaspoon vanilla paste or extract

Flaky sea salt, such as Maldon

1. In a medium nonreactive saucepan over medium heat, melt the butter and cook it until the foam subsides; don't brown it.

2. Add the sugar, vinegar, and vanilla, stirring to dissolve the sugar. Cook to a hard ball stage (260°F to 265°F on a candy thermometer for softer candy, 290°F to 300°F for brittle); do not stir. Watch the temperature carefully (see Tip).

3. Turn out the mixture onto a Silpat mat, lightly buttered sheet pan, or into silicone candy molds to cool about 30 minutes; sprinkle with sea salt to taste.

4. If you're not using candy molds, roll the candy out into about a ½-inch rope, then cut or pull it into bite-sized pieces about 2 inches long (you can pull and knead it like taffy if you want). Wrap each in wax paper to store. The candy keeps at room temperature for up to 1 month.

TIP

Make sure that your candy thermometer is not sitting on the bottom of the pan so you can get an accurate reading of the candy's temperature.

VINEGAR COMPOTE

MAKES ABOUT 2 CUPS

This is a great catch-all recipe for summer, when berries and other fruit are at their height of flavor and availability. I always seem to have two or three kinds of fruit around, and when they start to get soft, I make this. You can, of course, start with fresher fruit, but I always seem to turn to this recipe to preserve overripe fruit. You can use just about any fruit for this and really any vinegar— use a balsamic or red wine vinegar with berries for a more intense flavor, and lighter vinegars like white wine vinegar or rice vinegar with apricots or pears for a more delicate taste. Serve over yogurt, ice cream, or clabbered-milk blini (see page 110), or alongside lamb, goat, or roast beef. Don't forget to season your compote: black pepper is a great addition for strawberries and stone fruit; feel free to experiment with other spices, too.

2 cups berries or bite-sized pieces of fruit (anything other than citrus)

⅔ cup sugar

½ cup store-bought balsamic vinegar or homemade red wine vinegar (page 27), white wine vinegar (page 27), or any fruit vinegar (page 33), or store-bought

Pinch of salt

Freshly ground black pepper (optional)

1. In a medium bowl, combine the fruit and sugar and let the fruit macerate for at least an hour at room temperature, or even covered overnight in the fridge.

2. Mix the fruit and its juices with the vinegar in a medium nonreactive saucepan and simmer, uncovered, until the sauce thickens to the consistency of syrup or chocolate sauce; this could take as long as 20 minutes.

3. Add salt and pepper to taste, if desired. Serve the compote warm or cold. Store the compote in a tightly sealed container in the refrigerator for up to 2 months, or, to make it shelf stable, pour it into a clean pint-sized mason jar, screw on a lid and ring, and follow the steps on page 66 for water-bath canning.

CLABBERED-MILK BLINI
(PAGE 111)

ACKNOWLEDGMENTS

To my mom and dad, Marylyn and Harry, and brother, Aaron, who taught me to carry on more than one conversation at a time. To Taylor Erkkinen, my wife and partner in everything, for her support and for pushing me to write. And Moxie Ann and Mr. Frank, thanks for the laughs. And the hugs.

The excellent team at the Brooklyn Kitchen never complains about working with me and around my ever-growing experiments with vinegar and fermentation. You guys are the best.

To Angelin Borsics for making me into an author, and to Marysarah Quinn, Ed Anderson, Suzanne Lenzer, and Maeve Sheridan for making this book beautiful. Farley Chase's guidance was indispensable. And many thanks to the rest of the team at Clarkson Potter for their hard work, including Ada Yonenaka, Heather Williamson, Erica Gelbard, and Kevin Sweeting.

Many important ingredients, people, and places helped keep me going during the making of this book, including coffee, acetobacter, Michael Harlan Turkell, Heritage Radio Network, Claus Meyer, Bob Sewall, Eli Zabar, Sandor Katz, Ted Allen, Albert and Kim Katz, Andrea Bezzecchi, Justin Karr, John Karr, Nancy Singleton Hachisu, Yuko Suzuki, Bob McClure, Liz Thorpe, Jeremy Umansky, Patrick Martins, Talitha Whidbee, Neil Rosen, Neal Rosenthal, naptime, the Meat Hook, bourbon, gin, wine, cider, Laura Ingalls Wilder, Andy Swift, Lindera Farms, Keepwell, Christopher Nicolson, everyone who helped test these recipes, the Good Food Foundation, and the Good Food Retailer's Collaborative.

To all my friends, family, and neighbors, it truly does take a village.

Lastly, I'd like to take a moment to raise my glass to Steve Hindy and Garrett Oliver of the Brooklyn Brewery for working with and supporting so many of us who come to them with crazy ideas, such as my initial request to waste five gallons of their terrific product so that I could try my hand at making vinegar.

PERFECTING YOUR CRAFT

While making your own vinegar is very easy—requiring far fewer tools and steps than brewing beer or cider—there are ways to produce an even better product. This section breaks down a few complicated concepts into simple processes, from pasteurizing and clarifying batches to testing pH and acidity.

PASTEURIZATION

Pasteurizing is simply the process of heating the vinegar to 150°F in a nonreactive pot for 30 minutes, which kills any bacteria, molds, or yeasts, including acetobacter. The result is a shelf-stable product that you can store for an extended period of time. The vinegar is no longer "alive" and will not grow a mother—so it's ideal for bottling and gifting to someone who might be put off by the gelatinous mass. You can strain your vinegar through cheesecloth for more clarity before pasteurizing. However, I find that pasteurization weakens the flavors of the vinegar and decreases the healthful benefits of the fermentation. Since the bacteria needs oxygen to grow, you can instead just fill a clean bottle almost to the top and leave very little headspace. There won't be enough oxygen for the bacteria to thrive, leaving you with full-flavored and full-strength vinegar without heating or pasteurization. Your vinegar may grow a tiny mother in the bottle; this is often what you see in raw commercial vinegar where the mother has sunk to the bottom leaving sediment in the bottle.

ACHIEVING CLARITY

In some cases, depending largely on the chemical and mineral content of your starting product, your finished vinegar may still be cloudy. While I don't care about clarity, because it doesn't affect the flavor of vinegar, you may want a clearer vinegar when bottling for gifts.

To clarify your vinegar, there are a few steps you can take. I start with pouring or siphoning off the vinegar from anything that has fallen to the bottom of the barrel or jar where I'm fermenting. You will likely have sediment that has collected in the bottom; this is great for starting your next batch or giving to friends who want to join in on your acid trip. Cold helps clarity, and storing your vinegar in the fridge can help "cold crash" any sediments out of solution. Wait a few days and you'll be able to pour the clear vinegar off the sediment. You can also pour your vinegar through a coffee filter to remove any suspended mother or sediment. (It's a good idea to pour some boiling water through the filter first to sanitize it.)

DETERMINING PH AND ACIDITY

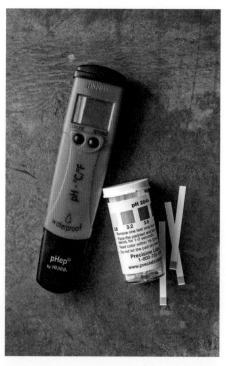

The pH (power of hydrogen) scale measures the concentration of hydrogen ions in a liquid to determine the relative acidity or alkalinity of a substance. The scale ranges from 0 to 14, with 7 being neutral (the pH of water is usually close to 7). The lower the pH level (i.e., anything below 7), the more acidic the ingredient; the higher the pH (i.e., above 7), the more basic or alkaline it is. Commercial distilled white vinegar (page 15) has a pH of 2.4 and 5 percent acidity, which means there are five parts acetic acid to ninety-five parts water.

In comparison, Coca-Cola has a pH of 2.53. A good rule of thumb is that the more tart and sour a vinegar tastes, the lower the pH and the higher the acid content. A pH test kit is a good and inexpensive investment for the home vinegar maker, as it will allow you to analyze and compare your ferments with one another. This is especially important if you're intent on processing pickled vegetable made with your homemade vinegar in a hot water bath—though I don't recommend it (store-bought vinegar is safest; for more information on canning, see page 66). The higher acidity also leads to more flavorful pickles.

Depending on the type of alcohol you use to make vinegar, you might end up with more than just acetic acid. Some of the common acids present in wine and cider include tartaric, citric, malic, lactic, ascorbic, and succinic. So while we can test the pH and get a proper measure of the acidity levels, you cannot be sure that the vinegar is purely acidic acid.

To test pH, you will need pH test papers or a pH meter (see Resources, page 153). The papers are cheap and not very accurate, but they will tell you the whole unit of the closest pH range. A pH meter will read to the hundredth place of pH, but it costs between $50 and $100 and requires calibration for best accuracy.

TESTING ACIDITY

To test for acid content, you will need an acid titration kit (see Resources, page 153) like the ones sold for wine making; they cost about $20. You will need to adjust your method, as the instructions contained will be for testing a much smaller percentage of acid in wine (usually 0.3 to 0.75 percent). Your titration kit should include the following:

- 20-milliliter syringe
- 150-milliliter testing cup
- 15-milliliter dropper bottle of indicator solution
- 100 milliliters of base liquid

Follow these instructions for testing the acid level in your vinegar:

1. Use the syringe to place 2 milliliters of vinegar in the testing cup. Add 20 milliliters of water and 3 drops of the indicator solution, and stir to combine.

2. Fill the syringe with 10 milliliters of the base liquid. Add the base, 1 milliliter at a time, until the liquid turns pink. Once the liquid

has turned pink, note how much of the base you added to get the reaction (for example, if you have 4 milliliters left in the syringe, then you used 6 milliliters of base).

3. Multiply the number of milliliters of base you added by 0.6; the result is the percentage of acid in your vinegar. So in this example, you would multiple 6 by 0.6 to get 3.6, or 3.6 percent acetic acid, which would taste tart like vinegar and be great for drinking or cooking with, but not acidic enough for canning.

ALCOHOL FERMENTATION

You can, of course, first produce your own wine, beer, or cider for making vinegar. If you're starting from scratch with the ultimate goal of vinegar, you can undertake a simultaneous fermentation. To do so, add the juice (for wine) or wort (for beer) to your vessel and sprinkle yeast over it. Add your mother and let the mixture sit, covered with a tea towel to prevent fruit flies. The yeast will convert the sugar into alcohol, and the acetobacter bacteria will convert the alcohol into acetic acid. Any juice containing sugar can be treated this way, such as apple cider or grape juice.

Use champagne yeast (see page 31) for the best results, as that will yield a very dry product without adding any yeast flavors. Most 5-gram packets of yeast are meant to convert 5 gallons of sugary liquid into an alcoholic beverage, so you'll need to adjust your yeast amount according to your quantity of base liquid.

AGING VINEGAR

To mellow the flavors of your vinegar, you can age it in the bottle or in a sealed crock or barrel for a year or more (no need to pasteurize it in order to do so). In some cases, aging vinegar will add oxidation, which adds depth of flavor as with port or sherry, and can smooth the acid kick. If you make a large batch of vinegar, set aside a bottle in the back of your pantry for a few years and taste it every few months to see how it changes over time. In China, Japan, and Korea it is not uncommon to find vinegars that age a minimum of three, five, or even seven years even before being bottled.

RESOURCES

I encourage you to seek out specialty-food, kitchen, and brewing-supply shops in your area and find out if they stock, or can get, any of the items you're looking for. You can also find most of the items listed at vinegarrevival.com or thebrooklynkitchen .com. And for your other vinegar-related questions, I am at your service and can be reached at 1-800-248-0513. Failing that, many of the items here can be found with a quick Internet search.

VINEGAR JUGS, POTS, AND BARRELS

Proper vinegar jugs and pots are easier to find in Europe than in the United States, but Ohio Stoneware makes a 2-gallon crock with a spigot that works well (ohiostoneware.com). When shopping for an oak barrel, look for the best quality you can find. You can buy one that's already been charred (typically sold for aging spirits) or plain oak. If you live near a craft distillery, ask if they're discarding any old barrels; ones that have aged spirits make perfect vinegar barrels. Querus Cooperage makes nice ones in New York state (qcooperage.com) or visit oakbarrelsltd .com or 1000oaksbarrel.com for a wide range of sizes and style.

PH METER AND STRIPS

Buy a real scientific meter, not a cheap knock-off. Hanna Instruments (hannainst .com) makes good ones.

JARS AND BOTTLES

Fillmore Container (fillmorecontainer .com) and SKS Bottle & Packaging (sks-bottle.com) are the best online sources. I like using Boston round bottles (also known as Winchester bottles) for storing and gifting vinegar.

HOMEBREW SUPPLIES, WINE THIEF, AND TITRATION TEST KITS

LD Carlson makes a simple titration kit like the one referenced on page 150. Any homebrew supply should have it or be able to order it for you, or you can find it online. LD Carlson does not sell direct to consumer.

CANNING TOOLS

Purchase a canning kit that contains all the essential tools (any of the Ball basic canning kits). A stainless steel funnel is better than plastic for handling hot liquids.

BOOKS

There are a few handy books (other than this one) that I would recommend reading:

Baiocchi, Talia. *Sherry*. Emeryville, CA: Ten Speed Press, 2014.

Katz, Sandor. *The Art of Fermentation*. White River Junction, VT: Chelsea Green Publishing, 2012.

Katz, Sandor. *Wild Fermentation*. White River Junction, VT: Chelsea Green Publishing, 2016.

Malle, Bettina, and Helge Schmickl. *The Artisanal Vinegar Maker's Handbook*. Austin, TX: Spikehorn Press, 2015.

Proulx, Annie, and Lew Nichols. *Cider*. North Adams, MA: Storey Publishing, 2003.

Turkell, Michael Harlan. *Acid Trip*. New York: Abrams, 2017.

SHOPS

Here are some of my favorite stores across the country that carry good-quality vinegar. Ask your local grocery store to stock it; chances are you're not the only customer who would buy it.

WEST

Healdsburg SHED
25 North Street
Healdsburg, CA 95448
healdsburgshed.com

Market Hall Foods
5655 College Avenue
Oakland, CA 94618
markethallfoods.com

Cowgirl Creamery
80 4th Street
Point Reyes Station, CA 94956
Ferry Plaza
and
One Embarcadero, No. 17
San Francisco, CA 94105
cowgirlcreamery.com

Bi-Rite Market
3639 18th Street
San Francisco, CA 94110
and
550 Divisidero Street
San Francisco, CA 94117
biritemarket.com

Canyon Market
2815 Diamond Street
San Francisco, CA 94131
canyonmarket.com

Liberty Heights Fresh
1290 1100 East
Salt Lake City, UT 84105
libertyheightsfresh.com

EAST

Each Peach Market
3068 Mount Pleasant Street, Northwest
Washington, DC 20009
eachpeachmarket.com

Glen's Garden Market
2001 South Street, Northwest
Washington, DC 20009
and
1924 8th Street, Northwest
Washington, DC 20001
glensgardenmarket.com

Washington's Green Grocer
8741 Ashwood Drive
Capitol Heights, MD 20743
washingtonsgreengrocer.com

Belfast Co-op
123 High Street
Belfast, ME 04915
belfast.coop

The Brooklyn Kitchen
100 Frost Street
Brooklyn, NY 11211
thebrooklynkitchen.com

The Greene Grape
767–769 Fulton Street
Brooklyn, NY 11217
greenegrape.com

Foragers Market
56 Adams Street
Brooklyn, NY 11201
and

300 West 22nd Street
New York, NY 10011
foragersmarket.com

Stinky Bklyn
215 Smith Street
Brooklyn, NY 11201
and
107 West 20th Street
New York, NY 10011
stinkybklyn.com

Eli's Market
1411 Third Avenue
New York, NY 10028
elizabar.com

Murray's Cheese
254 Bleecker Street
New York, NY 10014
(and other locations)
murrayscheese.com

Zabar's
2245 Broadway
New York, NY 10024
zabars.com

DiBruno Bros.
930 South 9th Street
Philadelphia, PA 19147
(and other locations)
dibruno.com

Woodstock Farmers' Market
979 West Woodstock Road
Woodstock, VT 05091
woodstockfarmersmarket.com

MIDWEST
Pastoral Artisan Cheese, Bread & Wine
2947 North Broadway Street
Chicago, IL 60657
(and other locations)
pastoralartisan.com

Zingerman's
422 Detroit Street
Ann Arbor, MI 48104
zingermans.com

Cooks of Crocus Hill
324 South Main Street
Stillwater, MN 55082
(and other locations)
cooksofcrocushill.com

Look's Market
6213 South Old Village Place
Sioux Falls, SD 57108
looksmarket.com

SOUTH
Antonelli's Cheese Shop
4220 Duval Street
Austin, TX 78751
antonellischeese.com

JM Stock Provisions
709 West Main Street
Charlottesville, VA 22903
and
1531 West Main Street
Richmond, VA 23220
stockprovisions.com

Taste
6464 Hampton Boulevard
Norfolk, VA 23508
(and other locations)
tasteunlimited.com

INDEX